How to Be a Super AI CPA

Unlocking the Power of Artificial Intelligence for Accounting Professionals

By

Craig Gordon

With

Irene Neumansky

Copyright © 2024 by Craig C. Gordon

All rights reserved.

No portion of this book may be reproduced in any form without written permission from the publisher or author, except as permitted by U.S. copyright law. To request permission, contact the publisher at the following address:

Attention: Permissions Coordinator
TD Publishing
365 Patteson Drive #115
Morgantown, WV 26505
www.tdfactfind.com

Author: Craig Gordon, Irene Neumansky
Editor: Sharen Kindel
Cover and interior design: Irene Neumansky
1st Edition: October 2024

TD PUBLISHING

This book is dedicated in memory to my father Richard C. Gordon Jr. CPA, Lehigh 1942 who taught his children life was more than just data and numbers.

Contents

Preface: The Urgent Call for CPAs in the Age of AI vii

Section 1 1

   1 Introduction and Who We Are 3
   2 How I Got to Teaching CPAs About AI 9
   3 Why You Should Become a Super AI CPA 17
   4 Why Understanding the Fundamentals of AI
      is Necessary 27

Section 2 33

   5 The 7 Rules for Understanding AI and Becoming a
      Super AI CPA! 35
   6 Rule 1: Why CPAs Need to Understand AI 47
   7 Rule 2: To Understand AI, One Must Understand the
      Definition of Intelligence 55
   8 Rule 3: Today's Reality Defines Current Intelligence
      and History Defines Current Reality 67
   9 Rule 4: Before Using AI Tools, CPAs Must Understand
      their Strengths and Weaknesses 75
  10 Rule 5: New Tools for CPAs in the Age of AI 87
  11 Rule 6: The Quest for AI Consciousness 97
  12 Rule 7: Ethical Foundations for Super AI CPAs 107
  13 Congratulations on Understanding AI and Becoming
      a Super AI CPA 117

Section 3 127

  14 What's Next to Stay a Super AI CPA 129
  15 Final Thoughts 137

Acknowledgments 143
Notes 147

Preface: The Urgent Call for CPAs in the Age of AI

THE ALARM BELLS ARE RINGING. The artificial intelligence revolution is upon us, and it's transforming our world at breakneck speed. But amidst all the hype and hysteria, there's a critical voice that's been conspicuously absent from the conversation: the voice of the CPA. That's right. CPAs are the unsung heroes of trust, verification, and financial integrity. And I'm here to tell you that your profession, your expertise, and your ethical grounding have never been more essential than they are right now.

As AI systems become more powerful and pervasive, they're raising profound questions about accountability, transparency, and oversight. Can we trust these machine learning algorithms to make fair and unbiased decisions? Are they open to feedback and correction when things go wrong? And who's minding the store to ensure these systems are auditable and adhering to standards of ethics and good governance?

These are the kinds of issues that keep coming up in panel after panel, from the hallowed halls of Davos to the cutting-edge labs of Silicon Valley. As Stanford professor James Landay puts it, "If a system makes a mistake and I can't correct that mistake or get feedback from the company, then I may not trust them in the future."[1] In other words, trust and verification - the very cornerstones of the CPA profession - are emerging as the key challenges in the brave new world of AI.

And it's not just academics who are recognizing this reality. The tech titans themselves are starting to wake up to the fact that AI isn't just about slick algorithms and fancy programming. As Jensen Huang, the visionary CEO of NVIDIA, recently observed, "Deep learning is a method. It's a new way of developing software."[2]

Think about that for a moment. The man who has done more than anyone to turbocharge the AI revolution is telling us that the real game-changer isn't the technology, but the methodology. What matters is the way we approach the development and deployment of these systems. And that methodology is about bringing domain expertise, critical thinking, and human judgment to bear on the AI challenge.

Consider what IBM's AI chief has to say on the matter: "Thanks to AI, you don't need a computer science degree to get a job in tech."[3] In other words, the skills that matter most in the AI economy won't necessarily be the ones that come out of a traditional STEM curriculum. Instead, they'll be the skills of insight, analysis, and integrity - the very skills that CPAs have been honing for generations.

What CPAs Do Really Well

Let's take a moment to reflect on your strengths:

- Trust and Verification: CPAs are trained to ensure that numbers add up, that processes are followed, and that financial statements reflect reality. This skill is vital in AI, where trustworthiness is paramount.

- Ethics and Accountability: Your profession demands a high ethical standard, making CPAs the perfect candidates to oversee AI systems and ensure they adhere to ethical guidelines.
- Numerical Analysis: Your expertise in analyzing complex data sets is directly applicable to working with AI, which thrives on data.

But here's the problem: even as the demand for your talents is skyrocketing, the CPA profession is at a crossroads. Enrollment in accounting programs has been plummeting[4], and people seem to think that being a CPA is boring, dull, and about as exciting as a root canal. Well, I'm here to tell you that nothing could be further from the truth.

As The Economist recently put it, "AI will not replace accountants. Instead, accountants who use AI will replace those who do not."[5] In other words, if you can learn to harness the power of these new technologies, you won't just be crunching numbers. You'll be at the forefront of shaping the future of finance, auditing, and business strategy.

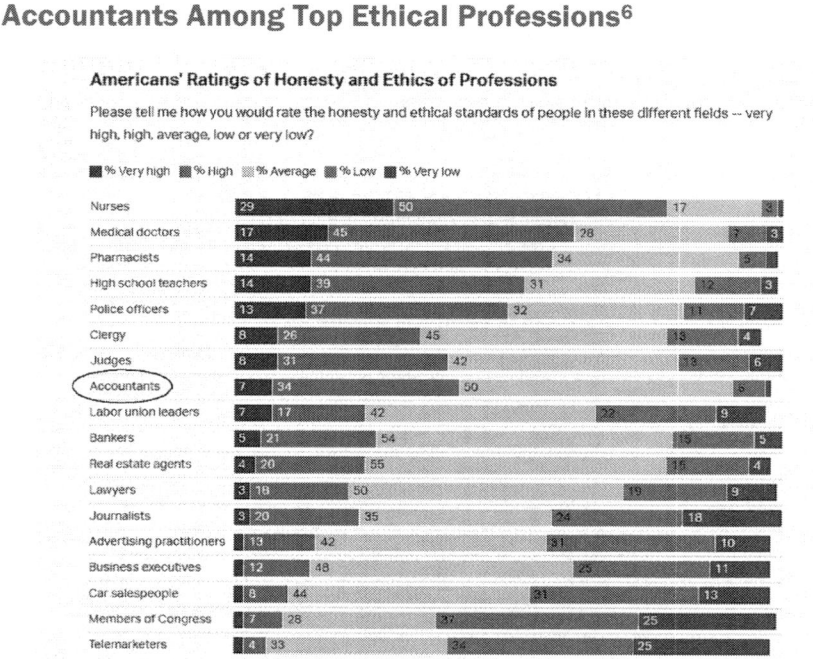

Accountants Among Top Ethical Professions[6]

Americans' Ratings of Honesty and Ethics of Professions

Please tell me how you would rate the honesty and ethical standards of people in these different fields -- very high, high, average, low or very low?

■ % Very high ■ % High ▨ % Average ■ % Low ■ % Very low

Profession	Very high	High	Average	Low	Very low
Nurses	29	50	17		3
Medical doctors	17	45	28	7	3
Pharmacists	14	44	34		5
High school teachers	14	39	31	12	3
Police officers	13	37	32	11	7
Clergy	8	26	45	13	4
Judges	8	31	42	13	6
Accountants	7	34	50		6
Labor union leaders	7	17	42	22	9
Bankers	5	21	54	15	5
Real estate agents	4	20	55	16	4
Lawyers	3	18	50	19	9
Journalists	3	20	35	24	18
Advertising practitioners	13	42	31	10	
Business executives	12	48	25	11	
Car salespeople	8	44	31	13	
Members of Congress	7	28	37	25	
Telemarketers	4	33	34	25	

Those with no opinion are not shown.
NOV. 9-DEC. 2, 2022

GALLUP

A Blueprint for CPAs in AI

This book is dedicated to providing you with a blueprint on how to become a pivotal player in the AI-driven landscape. By the end of this book, you will realize the immense competitive advantage that you have gained over those who remain uninformed about AI. You'll not only understand AI fundamentals but also how to apply them effectively in your profession.

This book is a framework - a set of 7 essential rules - for mastering the fundamentals of AI. Without resorting to jargon or technobabble, we will focus on the core concepts, the key challenges, and the vast opportunities that AI presents for CPAs who are willing to seize them.

Why is this foundational knowledge so critical? Because the AI landscape is evolving at warp speed. The generative language models and algorithmic techniques that are state-of-the-art today could be obsolete in a year or two. What you need is a bedrock understanding - a conceptual framework that will allow you to assess new developments, separate hype from substance, and apply the enduring principles of your profession to this brave new world.

So, if you're ready to turbocharge your career, future-proof your skills, and exert real influence over the development of AI, then this is the book for you. It will give you a profound competitive advantage over any CPA who hasn't taken this journey. You'll be armed with the knowledge and vision to become a true "Super AI CPA" - a trusted expert at the leading edge of your field.

Sound exciting? Then let's dive in. The future is coming fast, and it belongs to the CPAs who are ready to shape it. Turn the page, and let's get started on unlocking your AI superpowers.

Section 1

1

Introduction and Who We Are

LET'S TAKE A STEP BACK IN TIME. It's the late 19th century, and electricity has just burst onto the scene. People are abuzz with excitement, yet a bit skeptical. They see light bulbs, but they also hear about the occasional fire. Electricity was new, dazzling, and a bit mysterious.

Folks saw electricity's immediate potential – electric lights, telegraph machines, maybe even horseless carriages! But the really transformative, game-changing applications? Those were beyond anyone's wildest dreams. Sure, people could imagine electricity making existing tasks easier or replacing human labor in certain domains. But they couldn't yet conceive of the myriad ways it would reshape every facet of life.

Imagine transporting an average person from 1850 to 1925. In the space of seventy-five years, they'd go from a world lit by gaslight and powered by steam to one electrified by lightbulbs and wired for telephones. The pace of change would be dizzying!

But here's the thing: That time traveler, amazed as they'd be, would be equally struck to know about all the things electricity wasn't doing. No computers, no televisions, no microwave ovens. All those revolutionary applications were still decades away. The first electrical revolution was only getting started.

"Chatbot, please give me some examples of ideas for using electricity after it was first invented that were never developed, or were abandoned long ago"

Idea	Expectation/Goal	Problem/Reason Dropped
Electric Airships	Use electricity to power airships for transportation	Development of internal combustion engines and disasters like Hindenburg
Electrified Roadways	Vehicles receive power directly from road surface	Technical and safety challenges; battery-powered vehicles preferred
Electric Pens	Thomas Edison's idea: Duplicating documents through perforations	Overshadowed by more efficient mimeograph machines and photocopiers
Electrocuting Diseases	Use electricity to cure ailments	Ineffectiveness and unpleasant side effects
Food Preservation	Use electrical currents to kill bacteria or slow spoilage	Ineffectiveness; refrigeration became the preferred method

Fast forward to today. We can't imagine life without electricity. It powers our homes, our industries, our entire modern way of life. But it took visionaries to really harness electricity's potential - innovators who looked beyond the obvious applications and imagined whole new paradigms.

That's where we are today with AI. We're dazzled by the flashy applications – the self-driving cars, the eloquent chatbots, the algorithms that can spot cancer better than doctors[1]. But AI's real transformative potential, the stuff that will redefine what's possible? We've only scratched the surface.

And that's where we come in

We're a motley crew of AI enthusiasts from all walks of life. As for me, I'm a professor-turned-founder-turned-professor again. I've launched several market research companies and have been preaching the AI literacy gospel to business and journalism students for years. I'm on a quest to empower non-techies with a seat at the table. My partner in crime, Jeffrey Yudkoff, is a CPA with decades of experience, including stints teaching accounting at prestigious institutions like Yale University.

What unites us is a belief that AI is far too important to be left solely to software engineers and tech titans. It must be shaped by diverse voices, especially those who can see beyond the algorithms to grapple with its societal implications. And we're convinced that CPAs have an outsized opportunity – indeed a duty – to help ensure AI's transformative impacts unfold ethically, inclusively and in alignment with the public interest.

AI won't be limited to flashy projects coming out of big tech companies and research institutions. No. Like electricity, AI will seep into every nook and cranny of business and society, often in unexpected ways. And it will be pioneered not just by computer scientists, but by entrepreneurs, domain experts...and yes, even CPAs!

I'd argue CPAs are uniquely equipped to navigate the risks and rewards of AI. After all, CPAs combine deep business expertise with hard-earned credibility as trustworthy, impartial advisors. That skill set is tailor-made for the AI challenges ahead.

It all comes down to trust and verification. As AI permeates business, it will pose thorny questions about reliability, transparency, and ethics. Can we trust AI systems to be accurate and unbiased? How can we validate their decisions? What standards must they adhere to? And what processes and closed systems are too dangerous for businesses to use?

Tackling those challenges will require more than just technical know-how. It will demand the rigor, judgment, and professional skepticism CPAs bring to the table. Far from being tangential to the AI revolution, CPAs are uniquely equipped to shape it for the better. In a world where AI systems are making decisions, auditing the books, and predicting financial outcomes, the need for human experts to keep them honest has never been greater.

That's why we've poured our hearts into this book. We want to give you a roadmap to harness AI's potential in your own work. Our goal isn't to make you fluent in every last AI algorithm, though we'll certainly cover the key techniques. Rather, it's to instill in you a robust conceptual understanding and an audacious vision for your role in an AI-fueled world.

As practitioners grappling with AI's real-world implications, we've seen how it can uncover game-changing business insights. But we've also witnessed the pitfalls of chasing AI hype without a solid plan or a culture of accountability. We're convinced that CPAs unique blend of analytical prowess, professional integrity and domain expertise is the key to unlocking AI's full potential.

Throughout this book, we'll share stories, strategies, and wisdom to help you seize that potential. Trust us. This won't be your typical, by-the-numbers, accounting tome. We'll poke holes in conventional wisdom, examine provocative case studies, and pose the kinds of mind-bending questions that are key to thriving in an AI-centric future.

But we'll also ground every insight in the nuts-and-bolts realities of CPA practice, equipping you to become an indispensable strategic partner in navigating the brave new world of AI. Along the way, you'll gain facility with core AI concepts, learn to spot and counter algorithmic bias, develop techniques for auditing AI systems, and cultivate an innovator's mindset to keep you ahead of the curve.

By the time you reach the back cover, you'll be armed with a framework that puts you light years ahead of any CPA still stuck in the dark ages of AI ignorance. You'll have the knowledge to identify AI snake oil, devise high-impact applications, and guide your clients in harnessing AI's power responsibly. In short, you'll be a bona fide "Super AI CPA," ready to blaze new trails.

The AI future belongs to you – the trustworthy, knowledgeable, and ethically grounded professionals stepping up to keep artificial intelligence honest and aligned with the public good. And when the history books are written, you'll be the audacious accountants who were there from the start, keeping AI honest for the good of us all.

2

How I Got to Teaching CPAs About AI

I DIDN'T REALLY START OUT to teach AI to CPAs. Nor did I start by trying to sell anything to CPAs. My journey to this point began long ago with my background in education, marketing, and market research. This eventually led me to start multiple companies focused on innovative ways to conduct market research for the investment world.

My first business, Grassroots Research, started as an investigative research arm within an investment firm, providing a competitive edge through primary research and interviews. My second business, Off the Record Research (now OTR Global) used time series analysis for global market research projects. The firm's success led to marketplace checks being a must for all stock market investment professionals.

Around 2005, I realized that the world of market research was evolving. It was moving from primary, one-on-one investigative research to something new. A book called "The Fourth Paradigm," written by the head of Microsoft's R&D division, proposed that 99% of the questions we ask today already have answers hidden in existing data – the data is just discombobulated.

The book gave the example that the cure for a certain cancer might be found in some herb being used by an indigenous tribe in Brazil. While herbs may work for various cancers, that knowledge is isolated – no one else knows about it. In other words, the data is out there, but it isn't connected in a meaningful way.

The greatest real-world example of this concept was the discovery of the first effective AIDS drug[1]. Researchers were searching exhaustively for treatments, looking for drugs to halt the immune system collapse. They were coming up empty until one day, while combing through old test results, they found a failed colon cancer drug trial conducted by the University of Chicago.

The drug was supposed to decrease white blood cell counts, but white blood cell counts actually increased, as did the cancer's progression. The researchers realized the potential of a drug that could boost white blood cell counts for AIDS patients. This led to the first breakthrough treatment for HIV and AIDS.

The data to answer the AIDS riddle was already out there. It just wasn't coordinated in a meaningful way. This realization inspired me to start my third entrepreneurial venture, Blueshift Research, a company aimed at combining data with human checks to generate actionable market intelligence. But as I watched the evolution of the field, I eventually recognized, in mid-life, that I wanted to return to teaching.

As I began teaching again, I created a qualitative data analytics course at Lehigh University for journalism and marketing majors. It covered basics like Bayes' Theorem but applied to text rather than just numbers.

Around this time in 2016, I was also following the breakthroughs of Geoffrey Hinton in the field of artificial intelligence[2]. Looking at his work, I thought to myself, *I may not understand all the theory, but it sure seems like data analysis by itself is about to become obsolete. The next big leap will be artificial intelligence.*

I thought, if I was a smart 40-year-old, I'd start an AI company to ride that wave. But alas, I was no spring chicken. So, I did the next best thing: I started teaching AI to the next generation.

My colleague, Jack Lule, the chair of the journalism department at Lehigh, gave me an opportunity. He suggested I come teach

AI fundamentals to their freshmen and sophomore journalism students. His rationale was compelling: if AI was going to be as transformative as I believed, these students needed to understand it conceptually from the start of their education.

I began the course with Max Tegmark's Life 3.0[3] to paint a picture of where artificial intelligence was headed. Until around 2020, a lot of this still felt more like a pipe dream than a practical reality. You could see things starting to gather steam with innovations like large language models, but you still needed computer programmers to make it work. Access was tightly controlled by a small group of consumer and computer technology companies and chip manufacturers. Outside of that insular world, critical issues around the philosophy, ethics, and history of AI were largely being thrown by the wayside.

I began by teaching people to first understand intelligence itself, because they needed to be prepared for the emergence of non-human intelligence that could rival or surpass human capabilities. We studied the history of how our conception of intelligence had evolved over time and used that to project forward to how artificial intelligence might develop. A key focus was on defining intelligence and identifying tools that could be used to potentially mimic it. This formed the basis of what I taught in my introductory lecture classes. I wanted to give students a broad context to comprehend AI rather than just the technical nuts and bolts.

My longtime friend and collaborator Jeffrey Yudkoff, a CPA himself, took an interest in what I was teaching. "This is fascinating stuff," he said. "I'm doing all these routine continuing education courses, but I think you could get your course approved for CPAs. They should definitely be learning about this."

As I reflected on what Jeffrey said, I thought about my late father, who was a CPA. He loved numbers and was deeply committed to ensuring that the financial reports of the public company he worked for as CFO were a true and accurate representation of the company's reality.

Then it hit me: If you examine the pros and cons of artificial intelligence objectively, one of the first questions that comes up – and it's a huge one – is trust. How will we know if we can trust these AI systems? It dawned on me that CPAs, with their expertise in auditing and assurance, were the natural choice to tackle this challenge.

With this realization, Jeffrey and I went through the process of getting my course approved for CPA continuing education credits. As we explored the landscape of AI education for CPAs, we found that AI education for accountants was offered almost exclusively by two groups:

1. Computer science professionals within the Big Four firms
2. Companies selling AI-based accounting software

There was a glaring lack of AI training focused on conceptual foundations, societal implications and non-technical perspectives. CPAs were being taught which buttons to push, but not the underlying philosophies and human considerations. We sought to fill that gap.

Then in December 2022 the game changed virtually overnight with the release of ChatGPT. I vividly remember leading a beta test of our course with 16 people from Ernst & Young right after the news broke. I asked the group, "How many of you know what ChatGPT is?" No one raised their hand. I told them, "Within two years, you will all be using this." They looked at me in disbelief.

I realized that we needed to take a giant step back. The foundation of our course couldn't just be the latest flashy AI tool or technique. Who knows if large language models like ChatGPT would always be the bedrock? Spoiler alert! We don't think they will be.

Remember Chapter 1, where we compared AI's potential impact to the rise of electricity? We truly have no idea where this technology will lead us, just as early electrical pioneers could never have anticipated the full scope of changes electricity would bring about. The only thing we know for certain is that it will bring profound changes that are difficult to predict from our current vantage point.

This is precisely why understanding fundamentals is so essential. CPAs and accounting professionals cannot leave a development this consequential solely in the hands of computer science majors or profit-driven tech companies. We need to get multidisciplinary voices involved – liberal arts, philosophy, ethics. The business and domain expertise of fields like accounting are not just nice-to-haves. They are utterly essential to steering AI's development in a way that genuinely benefits humanity. CPAs have a central role to play.

I love the William Gibson quote, "The future is already here – it's just not very evenly distributed.[4]" CPAs have a critical role to play in shaping the future of AI in a way that preserves the core tenets of the accounting profession – trust, integrity, and transparency. By deeply understanding the philosophical underpinnings of intelligence and AI, CPAs can help ensure these technologies develop in an ethical, responsible, and accessible manner.

That's really the core purpose of this book. We're not here to sell you on any particular AI product or make a case for why one approach or piece of software is better than others. Our goal is simply to give you the foundational knowledge to ask the right questions, spot the key issues, and be an empowered advocate for the responsible development of artificial intelligence. We want to train you to think critically about what you're seeing and not get fooled by hype or surface-level claims.

In the coming years, AI will undoubtedly transform the accounting profession. It's not enough for CPAs to just learn which buttons to push in the latest software. You must be able to reason from first principles about the implications of artificial intelligence on your most essential function in society – providing assurance and lending credibility to important financial information.

The journey that led us here has been a long and winding one, with many pivots and revelations along the way. But the destination is clear – empowering CPAs to flourish and lead in the age of AI. The rest of this book will equip you with everything you need to know to become a "Super AI CPA." Let's get into it!

3

Why You Should Become a Super AI CPA

EMBRACING AI IS ABSOLUTELY CRUCIAL for CPAs. As artificial intelligence rapidly advances and transforms industries, accounting professionals who proactively engage with this technology will be positioned for incredible opportunities in the years ahead. By contrast, those who ignore AI's rise risk finding themselves at a severe competitive disadvantage.

This isn't just about jumping on the latest tech bandwagon or adding another tool to your digital toolkit. Grappling with AI goes to the very heart of what it means to be a trusted financial advisor and steward of the public interest in the 21st century. As AI systems grow more sophisticated, they raise profound questions around trust, transparency, and accountability – the very domains where CPAs' hard-earned credibility is most essential.

The impact of AI will be just as profound as the advent of electricity or the internet. And just like with those technological innovations, there are three key stages of adoption:

1. **Breakthrough Phase**: This is when the initial innovation happens, and a few brave souls – the early adopters – start to experiment with it.

2. **Early Adoption Phase**: Here's where the magic happens. Early adopters recognize the value of the technology and gain a competitive advantage over their peers. They become the trendsetters and thought leaders in their industries.

3. **Mass Adoption Phase**: By this point, the technology has proven its worth, and wider societal acceptance takes hold. Even the late adopters and laggards have to get on board or risk being left behind.

Compared to past technologies, AI is moving through these stages at warp speed. It's all over the press. Almost daily, we see examples of AI providing huge competitive advantages to early adopters. The question is, do you want to be an early adopter and gain that competitive edge, or do you want to play catch-up later on?

A Cautionary Tale:
The Old Reliable Smith CPA Firm

To illustrate this point, let's take a little trip down memory lane. Picture this: it's the 1960s and 70s, and we have two CPA firms – the "Old Reliable Smith CPA Firm" and the "Forward-Looking Jones CPA Firm."

The Old Reliable Smith firm is content to do things the way they've always been done. They're skeptical of newfangled "calculators" and "spreadsheets," worried they might create problems or compromise their work's integrity. They don't grasp the potential and prefer to stick to their tried-and-true methods, thank you very much.

But the Forward-Looking Jones firm, has a different perspective. They see these emerging technologies as powerful tools that can help them serve their clients better, faster, and more efficiently. They're not afraid to experiment and innovate, because they know that's how you stay ahead of the curve. They invest in learning about calculators and spreadsheets and start incorporating them into their practice.

Fast forward a few years, and guess which firm is thriving? That's right, Forward-Looking Jones. By embracing innovation early, they were able to gain a significant competitive advantage and better serve their clients.

The lesson here is clear: in the era of AI, you don't want to be an Old Reliable Smith. You want to be a Forward-Looking

Jones, always learning, experimenting, and leveraging new technologies to stay ahead of the curve. Embrace change and innovation, and you'll be the one reaping the rewards.

AI is a Tool. Not an Agent.

There's a lot of hype and speculation out there about AI taking over the world and rendering humans obsolete. But let me be clear: The AI we're talking about today is a tool, not an autonomous agent. It still requires human judgment, oversight, and interpretation to be used effectively.

In his book, "Co-Intelligence," Wharton professor Ethan Mollick[1] explains it this way: "A hammer is a tool that enhances our ability to build things, but it doesn't build the house for us." Similarly, AI can help us process and analyze data more efficiently, generate insights, and even assist with tasks like writing and problem-solving. But the AI of today still requires human oversight and understanding. It's not capable of replacing CPAs. Rather, it's here to augment and enhance your work.

As a CPA, you have a crucial role to play in the development and deployment of AI. You need to ensure the accuracy and integrity of the data being fed into these systems and provide the ethical guardrails and professional skepticism to keep AI in check. In short, CPAs need to be the human intelligence behind artificial intelligence.

From Data to Intelligence

One of the key things to understand about the current state of AI is how it handles the progression from raw data to actionable intelligence. Traditionally, humans have followed a three-step process:

Data → Information → Intelligence

We start with raw data. We process that data into meaningful information by applying context, judgment, and verification. Only then do we arrive at intelligence – insights and knowledge that can inform our actions.

AI, on the other hand, often skips that crucial middle step. It goes straight from data to intelligence, without the validation and contextualization that turns data into meaningful information. Since it lacks the inherent human ability to assess the data's reliability, relevance, and reasonableness, there's a significant chance it will make the wrong call.

Consider this example: If you ask an AI model to pick a random number between 1 and 100 multiple times, you might expect each number to come up roughly the same number of times. But in reality, you'll often see the number 42 pop up far more frequently. Why? As Mollick points out: Because the number 42 shows up a lot in the data the AI was trained on, such as pop culture references like "The Hitchhiker's Guide to the Galaxy,"[2] biblical references, and so on. AI models don't understand the contextual meaning of that number; they just know it shows up a lot.

That is where you, the human CPA, come in. Your job is to add meaning, trust, and accuracy to the data. It is your job to make sure that the step turning data into true information isn't skipped before it becomes intelligence. You are the crucial human oversight that ensures AI tools are being used effectively and ethically.

Practical Applications for CPAs

So, what does all this mean in practice? How can you, a CPA, start harnessing the power of AI today? There are tons of exciting possibilities, but here are a few key areas to consider:

- **Writing and Documentation:** AI-powered writing assistants can help draft reports, memos, and other documents more efficiently while ensuring consistency and compliance with standards. Natural language processing models can be used to make our writing more concise, persuasive, and reader friendly.

- **Brainstorming and idea generation:** AI can be a powerful tool for exploring new ideas and solutions. By analyzing vast amounts of data and spotting patterns, AI can help CPAs identify opportunities and innovative approaches you might not have considered otherwise.

- **Repetitive tasks:** Many accounting tasks, such as auditing, financial projections and data entry, involve repetitive processes that could be automated using AI. By leveraging AI to handle these tasks more efficiently, CPAs can free up time to focus on higher-level strategic work.

- **Anomaly detection:** AI excels at spotting unusual patterns or anomalies in data. This can be invaluable for identifying emerging trends, potential fraud, or areas that require further investigation. CPAs who leverage AI for anomaly detection can provide more proactive, insightful service to their clients.

These are just a few examples, but the possibilities are endless. The key is to approach AI as a tool to enhance your work, not as a replacement for CPA expertise. It's about harnessing AI's power to augment human judgment and oversight.

Now's the time for CPAs to roll up their sleeves and get their hands dirty. Play around with AI. And I'm talking to all of you – whether you're fresh out of school or seasoned partners. Most of the advances we see today are coming from people at all levels who aren't afraid to roll up their sleeves and experiment.

According to a May 2024 study by Microsoft and LinkedIn[3], senior partners and CEOs aren't the main power users of AI. It's actually the everyday workers who are really pushing the envelope. They're not waiting for someone to tell them what to do – they're diving in headfirst and figuring it out on their own.

But don't think the top brass isn't paying attention. Two out of three top executives said they wouldn't hire someone who doesn't have some working knowledge of AI! And you can bet that goes for hiring at CPA firms too.

Ethical and Philosophical Considerations

Of course, with great power comes great responsibility. As CPAs, you have a duty to use AI ethically and responsibly, always keeping the best interests of your clients and the public at the forefront.

Data accuracy and bias are critical concerns. As a society, we need to be vigilant about the quality and objectivity of the data we're feeding into AI systems to ensure that it is reliable, unbiased, and free from manipulation. Bad data leads to bad decisions. That's why we need robust processes for data governance and validation.

We need to be transparent about when and how we're using AI. We also need to be prepared to explain and justify the results. Blackbox algorithms that spit out answers with no context are a recipe for trouble. We need to strike a balance between leveraging the power of AI and maintaining the human judgment and accountability that are the hallmarks of the CPA profession.

Finally, we need to think proactively about AI's societal impact and work to ensure that it is developed and deployed in an ethical and equitable manner. As trusted advisors, CPAs have a key role to play in shaping the governance frameworks and best practices around AI.

These are weighty considerations, but they are also exciting ones that will require continuous learning, adaptation, and collaboration with experts from other fields. By embracing your role as ethical stewards of AI, CPAs can help ensure that this powerful technology is developed and used in ways that align with our values and benefit society as a whole.

Becoming a Super AI CPA

So that's the case for becoming more than a regular CPA – we call it becoming a Super AI CPA. It's not about chasing the latest fad or buzzword. Rather, it's about positioning yourself for success in a rapidly changing world. By embracing AI as a tool and learning to use it effectively, you can enhance the quality and scope of your work, provide more value to your clients, and cement your place as a trusted strategic advisor.

The competitive advantage for early CPA adopters is there for the taking, but it won't last forever. The time to act is now, and this book will help you become a Super AI CPA.

But don't just take my word for it. Start experimenting with AI tools yourself. Explore how they can enhance your work, improve your efficiency, and provide better insights for your clients. The more hands-on experience you gain, the better equipped you'll be to navigate this brave new world of AI-powered accounting.

Remember, becoming a Super AI CPA isn't about replacing human judgment with machines. It's about leveraging the power of AI to augment and enhance what CPAs do best – providing expert guidance, strategic insights, and ethical leadership to help our clients and organizations thrive.

Are you ready to embrace your inner Super AI CPA? Let's start shaping the future of accounting together!

"Chatbot, why are CPA's inputs important to the development of AI?"

Reason	Details/Rationale
Ethical Oversight	CPAs adhere to high ethical standards, guiding AI development to ensure responsible and ethical design and use
Risk Management	CPAs' expertise in identifying and managing risks is crucial for assessing AI implementation risks, including data security and privacy
Fraud Detection	CPAs' experience in spotting anomalies and suspicious activity can help train AI systems to detect fraud more effectively
Data Integrity and Governance	Establishing data governance frameworks, to ensure data used in AI systems is accurate, reliable, and ethically sourced
Audit and Assurance	Developing frameworks for auditing AI decision-making processes to ensure reliability and transparency as AI systems become more complex
Compliance and Regulation	Ensuring AI systems comply with relevant regulations

4

Why Understanding the Fundamentals of AI is Necessary

UNDERSTANDING AI isn't just a neat party trick – it could mean the difference between riding the wave of innovation and being left behind in the digital dust. Practically every day there's an announcement of a new way artificial intelligence is being used in the business world, a world that CPAs will have to oversee.

AI is advancing so fast that it can feel impossible to keep up. But if you ground yourself with a solid foundation in the basics, you'll be better equipped to make sense of each new breakthrough and steer the technology toward positive ends. It's like calculus. Once you wrap your head around core concepts, like integrals and derivatives, you hold the keys for unlocking the logic behind even the most mind-bending equations. Integrals tell the story of how an equation came to be, while derivatives give a glimpse into where the equation is headed. Without that base knowledge, you must rely on others to interpret the math for you. In short, you're left accepting the judgement of others.

AI fluency works pretty much the same way. Without a handle on the fundamental principles, you won't be able to ask the right questions or understand the rhyme or reason behind the lightning-fast changes. You'll be stuck taking the "experts" at their word.

Where to Start Climbing the AI Learning Curve

I used to suggest "Life 3.0" by Max Tegmark[1] for a conceptual understanding of AI's transformative potential. Tegmark's book is a great primer on the technical, philosophical, and societal dimensions we will need to grapple with as machines grow ever smarter. However, with the advent of chatbots and the ability to directly communicate with AI without programming, one really needs to know how to work with AI.

For the ultimate practical guide for weaving AI into your professional life effectively and ethically, reach for "Co-Intelligence." Mollick's book distills the essence of human-machine collaboration down to four rules that I believe every CPA should tape to their monitor[2].

Mollick's Rules

1. **Invite AI into Business Discussions**: Don't relegate AI to some isolated silo – make it a core part of your strategic conversations and decision-making. Ask it the tough questions. The more you engage the models, the better you'll grasp their quirks and capabilities.

2. **Remember That You're the Human and it is Not**: It's easy to get swept up in AI's human-like qualities, but don't forget that behind the witty banter is a bunch of clever code. Its outputs can be biased, inconsistent, or just plain wrong. Applying your hard-earned domain knowledge and professional judgment is essential for keeping AI on track.

3. **Treat AI Like a Human**: Even though AI is not human, you still should treat it as one. And, to get the most out of AI, assign it a specific role, like a fellow CPA, client, or subject matter expert. The clearer the parameters, the better the output.

4. **The Best is Always Yet to Come**: The AI you use today will be the worst version you ever use. It's only going to get better, faster, and smarter, so plan for exponential advancement and stay nimble.

Make it a habit to attend conferences, webinars, and workshops on accounting and artificial intelligence. We think this is so important that we run artificial intelligence update seminars almost every other month! Follow thought leaders who can translate between the technical and business worlds. Keep a learning mindset and be brave about experimenting with AI tools in controlled sandboxes.

The more you learn about AI and how it works, the better you'll be at imagining new uses, spotting scams, and predicting unintended impacts. Being fluent in AI will be essential for any finance leader who wants to stay ahead of the curve.

A Framework for AI Mastery

We've covered why understanding the foundation of AI is so important and we've given you some suggested reading to get you started. But what does that learning journey actually look like? The rest of this book will equip you with a framework for understanding the AI landscape through an accounting lens.

By the time we're done, you'll have a solid understanding of AI's past, present, and future. You'll be grounded in the technical details and (hopefully) inspired by a sense of purpose and possibility.

The CPA's Role in AI Development

Let's zoom back out for a minute. The accounting profession has always provided clarity and assurance in an uncertain world. You help companies make sense of their finances, verify their current practices, and plan for the future.

4 | WHY UNDERSTANDING THE FUNDAMENTALS OF AI IS NECESSARY

As artificial intelligence shapes the business world, that mission is more important than ever. AI will bring new complexities and risks that need a CPA's careful eye – from biased algorithms baking in unfairness, to automated systems no one fully understands.

I know some of you might be worried about AI's limitations and potential downsides. You're right to be concerned. Let me give you a historic example to show why relying on experts in only one field to develop AI could be a problem.

Take Isaac Newton, the undeniable genius who discovered gravity. People saw him as an expert in everything and asked him all sorts of questions outside his field. But he spent a lot of his life trying to turn lead into gold. Spoiler alert: he never succeeded. The lesson is clear: having an expertise in one area doesn't necessarily make you an expert in others.

More recently, we've seen the problems that develop when new technology is left unchecked by outside views. The social media giants are still doing damage control for their roles in eroding privacy, spreading misinformation, and mental health harms. They moved fast and broke important things!

The good news is you're far better prepared to handle this new territory than you might think. The same skepticism and strong ethics that have always defined accounting are exactly what we need to help guide AI. However, you need a framework, a methodology to help you apply those principles to this new field. That's precisely what the rest of this book aims to provide.

We have taken an unbiased, product-neutral approach. Our goal isn't to sell you on the latest and greatest AI tools but to give you the knowledge you need to confidently go toe-to-toe with the world's tech geniuses – or at least your firm's AI specialists.

As a CPA, you bring a unique and valuable perspective to the AI conversation. Your expertise in trust, verification, business problems, and processes is essential for ensuring responsible AI development. It's time to claim your seat at the table.

Section 2

5

The 7 Rules for Understanding AI and Becoming a Super AI CPA!

WE'VE LAID THE GROUNDWORK for why CPAs need to understand AI. Now it's time to dig into the meat and potatoes -- the seven rules that will transform you from an ordinary numbers-cruncher into a Super AI CPA.

35

These seven rules are the distilled wisdom from years of teaching AI concepts to non-techies, combined with the hard-earned insights of veteran CPAs like my buddy Jeffrey. These seven rules are your roadmap to thriving in the AI revolution that's reshaping the world.

Why seven rules? Well, why not? After all, seven is a lucky number. But more importantly, these seven areas cover everything a forward-thinking CPA needs to know about AI. Let's start with a quick tour of what you will learn in subsequent chapters, along with some real-world examples that will help these concepts stick in your brain. Don't worry if some of this sounds a bit strange. For now, just focus on getting a feel for the big picture.

The Seven Rules

1. Why CPAs Need to Understand AI (And Why AI Needs CPAs!)
2. To Understand AI, You Must Understand Intelligence
3. Today's Reality Defines Current Intelligence, and History Defines Current Reality
4. Before Starting to Use AI Tools, Understand Their Strengths and Weaknesses
5. New Tools for CPAs in the Age of AI
6. The Quest for AI Consciousness
7. Ethical Foundations for Super AI CPAs

Rule 1: Why CPAs Need to Understand AI (And Why AI Needs CPAs!)

First things first: Why you should care about AI. It's not just about keeping up with the latest tech trend. It's about understanding that AI is going to revolutionize accounting, and you want to be at the front of that change.

But AI needs you, just as much as you need it. Why? Because AI has a trust problem, and trust is a CPA's superpower. When a CPA puts their stamp of approval on something, people sit up and take notice. It's a seal of quality that says, "Hey, you can trust this."

Here's a real-world example that really drives this home. Picture this: You're a business owner walking into a bank, looking for a loan. You've got your financial statements all prepared, and you're feeling confident. The banker takes a skeptical glance at your documents and says, "Hmm, interesting." But now, imagine you've got a CPA by your side, vouching for the accuracy of those statements. Suddenly, the bank's confidence shoots through the roof!

That is the power of CPA trustworthiness. And as AI starts making more and more critical decisions, we, the users of AI, are going to need that same level of trust.

Rule 2: To Understand AI, You Must Understand Intelligence

This might seem obvious but stick with me here: Before we can wrap our heads around artificial intelligence, we need to understand what plain old intelligence is.

Think about it: Before creating an artificial flavor, you need to know what real flavor is like, right? Same goes for artificial colors, or artificial anything. So why should AI be any different?

In this book, we will divide intelligence into six key components:

1. Engaging with reality
2. Memory and knowledge
3. Rational and logical thinking
4. Learning new things
5. Emotions beyond logic
6. Connectedness or spirituality

Understanding these components of intelligence will help us see where AI shines and where it falls flat. And that's key to knowing how to use AI in your work.

Here's a practical example: Imagine you're working in customer support and a frustrated client calls in, shouting, "I hate your product!" A human representative would pick up on the emotion in that statement, understanding that "hate" implies strong negative feelings that might lead to other emotions or actions.

An AI system, on the other hand, might just tag "hate" as a negative word and completely miss the emotional weight behind it. It might not understand that this customer needs extra care and attention to prevent them from canceling their service or badmouthing the company to others.

This example shows why it's important for CPAs to understand both the strengths and limitations of AI. You need to know when AI can enhance your work, and when the human touch is irreplaceable.

Rule 3: Today's Reality Defines Current Intelligence, and History Defines Current Reality

This rule asks that we take a step back and look at the big picture. To really understand AI, we need to understand how intelligence changes over time. And to do that, we need to look back at human history.

Mark Twain said that "history doesn't repeat itself, but it often rhymes."[1] I love that quote because it captures how looking to the past can help us navigate the future, even if the details are different.

When it comes to major technological revolutions, we usually see the following pattern, enumerated by Ray Kurzweil[2].

1. Initial Excitement: "Wow, this is amazing!"
2. Reality Check: "Uh oh, we didn't think about these problems…"
3. Adaptation: "Okay, now how do we fix this?"

We saw it with the telephone, the internet, and now we're seeing it with AI. At first, everyone is excited about the possibilities. Then the problems start cropping up – privacy issues, biases in the algorithms, unintended consequences. And finally, we buckle down and start working on solutions.

This is where CPAs come in. You're trained to ask the tough questions and not get swept up in hype. That's what makes you perfectly suited to be the voice of reason in a room full of AI cheerleaders.

When everyone else is caught up in the "Wow" phase, you can be the ones asking, "But what about...?" When others are stuck in the "Uh-oh" phase, you can be the ones saying, "Okay, how do we fix this? How do we make it work?"

For example, when a new AI-powered financial tool comes out, a tech company might focus on how fast it can process transactions. But a CPA might ask, "How does this tool ensure data privacy? What happens if it makes a mistake? How can we audit its decisions?" These are the kinds of questions that need to be asked to ensure that AI is developed and used ethically and responsibly.

By bringing a critical eye to AI developments, CPAs can help steer the technology towards more responsible and effective use.

Rule 4: Before Using AI Tools, Understand Their Strengths and Weaknesses

Now we're getting into the nitty-gritty. AI tools are popping up left and right, and each one is promising to revolutionize how we work. It's tempting to jump on every shiny new gadget. But before you start using AI in your practice, you need to have a clear understanding of what these tools can and cannot do.

Remember, no AI tool is a magic wand that can do everything. Each one has its strengths and limitations. Your job as a Super AI CPA is to know which tool to use for which job, and when human expertise needs to take the wheel.

We'll get into this in more detail in chapter 9, but for now, here are a few examples of how the right AI tool can help you work smarter:

Data Analytics: AI is fantastic at spotting trends in large datasets, but the predictions are only as good as the data they're based on. AI's predictions may not be able to account for unprecedented events or nonstop changes in the business environment.

Automated report generation: The right AI tool can quickly generate routine reports, saving you time. But human oversight may be needed to ensure that these reports make sense for specific stakeholders.

Natural Language Processing: AI is great for analyzing large volumes of text data, like contracts or financial reports. But it might miss context or sarcasm that a human would easily pick up.

By understanding the strengths and weaknesses of each AI tool, you'll know when to use them and when to rely on your own expertise.

Rule 5: New Tools for CPAs in the Age of AI

AI is opening up a whole new toolbox for CPAs, and the possibilities are mind-blowing. But some of the most game-changing applications seem to be coming from unexpected places.

My advice? Experiment, experiment, experiment! Don't be afraid to think outside the box and try things that, at first, might seem a little crazy. And don't be discouraged by the so-called "experts." The field of AI is so new and fast moving that there really aren't many true experts. How can there be, when we're dealing with a technology that's constantly changing?

Your hands-on experience with financial data and business processes might lead you to discover an AI application that no computer scientist would have thought of.

Maybe you will develop an AI tool that can predict cash flow with incredible accuracy. Or an audit assistant that can spot fraud in real-time. Or a system that can keep track of ever-changing financial regulations and flag compliance issues.

The key is to approach these possibilities with an open mind and a willingness to learn. And when you stumble onto something that works, share it with your peers! The more we collaborate and build on each other's discoveries, the faster we'll advance the field of AI in accounting.

Rule 6: The Quest for AI Consciousness

Now, you may be thinking, "AI consciousness? Isn't that a bit out there for us numbers-crunchers?" Well, yes and no. While

CPAs might not be on the front lines of developing conscious AI, I promise you, considering it is relevant.

Current thinking is that for AI to truly match human intelligence, it needs to develop some kind of consciousness. This means experiencing things like pleasure, pain, and wisdom, and grappling with concepts like mortality.

We're in uncharted territory here. We don't really know if machine consciousness is possible, or what it would look like if it were. But as a CPA, you need to know about these discussions. They'll help you ask better questions and make smarter choices about using AI in your work.

For instance, if an AI system is making financial decisions, we might need to understand its "reasoning" process. Does it have any concept of ethics or long-term consequences? Can it explain its decisions in a way that makes sense to humans?

While you may not be directly involved in creating AI consciousness, being aware of these discussions can help you ask better questions and make more informed decisions about the use of AI in your work.

As AI continues to advance, don't be surprised if you find yourself wrestling with some profound questions about the nature of intelligence and decision-making. It's all part of the journey to becoming a Super AI CPA!

Rule 7: Ethical Foundations for Super AI CPAs

Last but definitely not least, we need to talk about ethics. As AI tools become more powerful and pervasive, we need rock-solid ethical frameworks to make sure they're built and used the right way.

Unlike many other fields, including computer science, CPAs already have a strict code of ethics[3]. The whole profession is built on integrity, objectivity, and looking out for the public good. We need to bring that same level of ethical thinking to AI.

Think of your ethical code as a starting point for developing AI ethics in finance. Just as you have rules for staying independent, protecting client confidentiality, and acting in the public interest, we need similar guidelines for AI systems.

Some questions to consider:

- How do we ensure AI systems are making fair and unbiased decisions?
- What level of transparency should we require in AI-powered financial analysis?
- How do we balance the efficiency gains of AI with the need for human oversight and accountability?
- What safeguards need to be in place to protect sensitive financial data used in AI systems?

Remember, ethics isn't just about following rules, it's about instilling values at every level: individual, group, and more broadly community. As you work with AI, be sure it is being used responsibly and for the greater good.

Your Roadmap to Becoming a Super AI CPA

There you have it - a whirlwind tour of the seven rules that will guide your transformation into a Super AI CPA. Some of this might seem a bit abstract right now, but don't worry. We will dig much deeper into each rule in the coming chapters.

The big takeaway here is that becoming a Super AI CPA isn't just about learning to use new tools. It's about changing how you think. It's about *reimagining what it means to be a CPA in a world full of AI.*

So, as we move forward, keep an open mind. Be curious. Ask lots of questions. Don't be afraid to experiment. And always, always let your ethical compass guide you. The future of accounting is being written right now, and with these rules in your pocket, you'll be ready to help write that story.

Now let's roll up our sleeves and dig into each of these rules.

6

Rule 1: Why CPAs Need to Understand AI

AI IS MORE THAN JUST A COMPUTER PROGRAM, it's a deep learning machine.

Let's start with that most critical of all questions: Why should accountants and CPAs care about AI? I mean, isn't this stuff just for the computer geeks and tech bros? The answer is a resounding no!

Let me share an example. We recently did an interesting exercise with ChatGPT. We said "Hey Chatbot, imagine you're the owner of the Twinkies® Cupcake Company[1] trying to keep your business afloat. How would you submit a proposal to dietitians for a Type 2 diabetes daily meal regime?" Here's Chat GPT's response:

"Stress the importance of balance, moderation, and education. Highlight your commitment to tweaking the classic recipe to suit a health-conscious lifestyle. Twinkie Cupcakes can still be on the menu for those managing Type 2 diabetes, provided they are consumed wisely and as part of a diet that's aligned with healthy living principles."

Chuckle with me here, but would you ask the Twinkie Cupcake Company for advice about managing diabetes? Probably not. That's not their business. They just want to sell snack cakes!

AI: The Deep Learning Machine

When it comes to artificial intelligence, we, as a society, are quick to treat computer scientists, consumer tech companies, and programming wizards as the ultimate authority. But AI is much bigger than what the techies would have you believe. AI isn't a fancy computer program or an algorithmic magic trick. No, my friends. AI is a deep learning machine that's rapidly evolving to tackle all sorts of complex tasks – including many in the accounting and finance realm. And as AI gets smarter and more sophisticated, it's going to become an increasingly powerful tool in the hands of businesses and individuals alike.

But here's the thing: If we leave the development and deployment of AI solely to the tech geeks and software engineers, we risk ending up with systems that may be technically brilliant but ethically dubious or financially reckless. Just as you wouldn't trust the Twinkie Company to devise a nutrition plan for diabetics, we can't afford to let narrow tech interests monopolize something as transformative as artificial intelligence. To truly grasp its potential and pitfalls, we need to bring a much broader range of perspectives to the table.

That's where you come in, my CPA friends. With your hard-earned expertise in financial analysis, risk assessment, auditing and more, you have a vital role to play in shaping the future of AI. With your professional skepticism and real-world knowledge, you can help ensure that AI systems are not only effective but also trustworthy, transparent and aligned with sound accounting principles.

Your profession brings a critical lens of trust, verification, and financial expertise that is desperately needed in the AI conversation. Thanks to AI, said Matthew Candy, IBM's AI leader, you might not need a computer science degree to get a job in tech anymore[2]. IBM, we hear, is now proactively seeking people with diverse skills and thinking styles – accountants, writers, even musicians. This is bigger than computer science. Imagine how different social media would look if we had involved more than just tech firms from the start. There's a real risk in over-relying on programmers simply because AI involves code.

Now, you may be thinking that you didn't become a CPA to fiddle around with computer code! And sure, you don't need to become a coding whiz to stay relevant in the age of AI. But just as you wouldn't perform an audit without understanding double-entry bookkeeping, you can't afford to be AI-illiterate in a world where machine learning is rapidly reshaping the business landscape.

To contribute meaningfully, you first need a solid grasp of the fundamentals. What do we mean when we say AI? There are three main types:

1. Narrow or Weak AI - This is AI that's focused on one specific task, like Siri's voice recognition or those snazzy self-driving cars. It's impressive but limited in scope.

2. General AI - Now we're talking about AI that can juggle multiple tasks at once, more akin to human intelligence. Like a Roomba that doesn't just mindlessly vacuum but maps your room dimensions and could even suggest feng shui furniture arrangements!

3. Super AI - This is the wild card. Super AI doesn't just mimic human intelligence, it blows it out of the water. Some predict we could have Super AI within minutes of achieving general AI, while others estimate decades. It's a hugely debated timeline.

As you expand your AI knowledge, you'll encounter a bunch of jargon, everything from machine learning to neural nets, and large language models. Let's break it down and give you a clear framework to help you make sense of it all.

Think of the major AI models like GPT, Gemini, Wu Dao 2.0, and others as different "languages" of AI, each with their own quirks and capabilities based on how they were developed. Some, like Google's DeepMind® and OpenAI's GPT, are described as closed source, meaning their code is secret and they're ultimately driven by corporate profit motives. Others, like the open-source Mistral AI's Large 2 and Facebook's llama 3.1 aim to be more transparent and grounded in humanistic principles. China's Wu Dao, meanwhile, is shaped by centralized state goals that go beyond pure profit.

But what happens if those datasets are full of biases, blind spots or bugs? As they say in the software world, garbage in, garbage out. An AI trained mainly on the musings of male, western, 21st century netizens is going to have some big holes when it comes to representing humanity's true intellectual diversity.

Many of the most game-changing innovations are happening in unlikely places, beyond established infrastructures. Just as VHS, an inferior technology, beat out Betamax to become the dominant format, CPAs have a role to play to ensure that AI standards and practices are based on something other than purely profitable goals.

And what about those proprietary models being cooked up by for-profit tech titans and authoritarian regimes? If an AI's function is to maximize shareholder value or government control, you can bet we're in for some dystopian unintended consequences.

This is precisely why we need professionals like you, the CPAs, to lend your expertise to the AI conversation. Because at its core, your profession is all about trust and verification. You're trained to sniff out when the numbers don't add up, to hold organizations accountable, and to uphold rigorous standards. We desperately need that kind of scrutiny in the AI arena.

Trust and verification will be key CPA competitive advantages in the age of AI, along with domain expertise, pattern recognition, and a deep understanding of how to ask the right questions. The era of enlightenment that we've had for the past few centuries is giving way to the era of "entanglement," where success depends on integrating knowledge from different fields and true rewards await those who can bridge multiple realms of expertise. CPAs who embrace this will futureproof their careers.

Looking ahead, I see a huge opportunity for accountants who jump on the AI train early. You already have deep knowledge and trusted relationships with clients. By getting savvy with AI, you can offer even more value, from ongoing audits to real-time strategic advice. Early adopters will gain a massive competitive edge.

As AI continues to evolve from narrow to general to maybe even super-intelligent systems, I urge you to remain ever curious and critical. Don't just take Silicon Valley's word for it. Question their assumptions, poke holes in their logic, and demand a seat at the table.

With AI in your toolkit, you'll uncover creative solutions to age-old problems and find patterns and insights that manual methods would miss. You could even develop your own AI systems, infused with the integrity that defines accounting. Of course, there will be challenges. Bias and groupthink can creep into data and algorithms. Game-changing breakthroughs often come from outside the establishment.

Now imagine, a CPA approved version of a generative AI language model being adopted by a fortune 500 company vs. a non-CPA approved version. Which one do you think will be selected?

By expanding AI fluency, practicing healthy skepticism, and leading critical conversations, CPAs can help keep AI on an ethical and productive path. The journey won't be easy. Nothing worthwhile ever is. But the destination – a world where artificial and human intelligence work together for the greater good – is worth every bit of effort.

The future of AI is just too important to be left solely in the hands of the programmers and tech titans. We need ethicists and artists, skeptics and dreamers, guardians of truth like CPAs to ensure this technology benefits all of humanity. If we want AI to become a force for good – a tool that enhances human potential rather than displacing or diminishing it – we're going to need the steady hands and keen minds of accounting professionals guiding the way at every turn. So roll up your green visors, sharpen your pencils, and get to work. The future depends on you.

7

Rule 2: To Understand AI, One Must Understand the Definition of Intelligence

LET'S TALK ABOUT one of the most important questions in our quest to create artificial intelligence: what exactly is intelligence? We're all impressed by the latest AI gadgets the tech geniuses keep churning out, but have you ever stopped to think about what is meant by the word intelligence?

Intelligence isn't just some vague, academic concept. It is at the heart of what makes us human, and what we're trying to build into machines. But for all our IQ tests and brainy feats, we still don't have a clear, consensus definition of what intelligence really is.

Over the ages, some of the greatest minds have taken a crack at defining intelligence. Some of these thought-provoking attempts include:

> "Intelligence is the ability to accomplish complex goals." - Max Tegmark[1]

> "I know that I am intelligent because I know that I know nothing." - Socrates[2]

> "Intelligence is the ability to adapt to change." - Stephen Hawking[3]

> "I'm grateful to intelligent people. That doesn't mean educated. That doesn't mean intellectual. I mean intelligent." - Maya Angelou[4]

> "The true sign of intelligence is not knowledge but imagination." - Albert Einstein[5]

> "To acquire knowledge, one must study; but to acquire wisdom, one must observe." - Marilyn vos Savant[6]

Each of these folks is onto something, but we need to dig a little deeper. The way I see it, any useful definition of intelligence needs to include at least six key elements:

7 | RULE 2: TO UNDERSTAND AI, UNDERSTAND INTELLIGENCE

1. Engaging with reality
2. Memory and knowledge
3. Rational and logical thinking
4. Learning new things
5. Consciousness and emotions beyond just logic
6. Connecting with other living things and the world around us

Let's break each of these down and explore what they mean for the future of Artificial Intelligence.

Reality Check

First up, intelligence isn't just about what's in your head, it's about how you engage with the world around you. But reality changes. It depends on when and where you live.

Think about it. The world of someone from the 1800s is totally different from what we experience today. Back then, our understanding of the world grew in a steady, linear progression. But the world of the 21st century isn't following that age-old pattern. Our world is experiencing a logarithmic explosion of knowledge! Advances that used to take centuries are now happening every decade, sometimes even faster. This means that both humans and AI systems need to constantly figure out what data is still relevant and what's become obsolete.

Imagine if we'd just stuck with the idea that everything revolves around the Earth, or that the world is flat. We'd have missed out on a whole universe of knowledge – literally! It's the same in business. Whenever someone says, "That's just the way it's done," it's a sure sign that we need to dig deeper and question assumptions.

Now consider AI's "reality." AI systems only see the slice of the world we feed it through data and tasks. An AI that's a champion at chess knows nothing about the complex real world we navigate every day. Understanding just how colorful and messy human reality can be is step one in seeing the difference between the AI we have now and the kind that could really think like a person. As we look at AI's progress, we have to keep asking: is it actually engaging with reality at a human level? Or is it just a really clever machine in a simplified world?

Are you starting to see why CPAs might be indispensable in developing and using AI tools? You can help ensure that AI systems don't get stuck in outdated ways of thinking, but instead evolve along with our expanding understanding of the world. Your ability to question assumptions, provide context to raw data, and adapt to changing realities – these are superpowers in the age of AI. How's that for job security!

Mastering Memory

Next up, let's talk about memory. And I don't mean just storing a bunch of information – computers have always been great at that.

Human memory is much richer than that! When we remember something, it's often not just dry facts, but a mix of emotions, connections, and experiences. It's why an old song

7 | RULE 2: TO UNDERSTAND AI, UNDERSTAND INTELLIGENCE

can flood you with nostalgia, even if you can't remember what you had for breakfast.

Compare that to AI memory, which is just 1s and 0s. An AI can recite a textbook word-for-word, but it doesn't have a personal connection to that information. It doesn't link those facts to pride, or embarrassment, or any other human feeling.

So, when an AI shows off its amazing recall, remember that your memory is tied to judgment and experience in ways AI can't (yet) match.

Logical Thinking: The Software of Smarts

Let's talk about what most folks think of as intelligence – logic and reasoning. And sure, being able to solve problems is a big part of being smart.

Computers have always been amazing at cranking through calculations and following complicated rules. But real-world reasoning – the kind we use in relationships, business deals, or crafting arguments – is way messier.

Why? Because human thinking is full of quirks, biases, and mental shortcuts. We don't just analyze - we use intuition, emotion, and gut feelings.

Plus, people have a kind of meta-thinking – we can reason about our reasoning, spot holes in our logic, and change our beliefs based on new information.

Today's AI is great at solving clear-cut problems. But when things get fuzzy, it can stumble. To really match human smarts, the next wave of AI can't just solve pre-programmed problems.

It has to be able to take on those head-scratcher problems where step one is working out what the question even is – the part that's mixed up with intuition, imagination, and good old common sense.

Learning is the Key to Intelligence

The mark of real intelligence is the ability to grow and change as you go. And AI has made some incredible leaps here in recent years!

With machine learning, AI systems can now spot patterns, make guesses, and improve themselves with little human intervention. Fed enough examples, an AI can learn to recognize faces, translate languages, and even beat humans at games of strategy.

But there's a catch: The learning we're seeing from today's top-of-the-line AI systems is still pretty narrow and brittle. An AI trained to master chess can't transfer that know-how to driving a car or writing a sonnet. It's like a student who's crammed for one test, but clueless about other subjects.

Human learning, on the other hand, lets us use what we know all over the place. Think how easily kids soak up knowledge about the world. Just by exploring and interacting, they learn concepts and skills that they can apply to all sorts of new situations. Their learning extends beyond any one domain. That's because human learning is tied up with things like emotion, motivation, identity, and open-ended curiosity – the drive to explore, to play, to ask "what if?"

As AI gets smarter, it may need to learn more like we do – not just be crammed with facts but understand curiosity and how to play around with ideas just for fun.

Consciousness: The Magic Spark

Here's where things get really wild. Human thoughts and experiences are drenched in feelings, wants, and self-awareness. We don't just think, we feel. We are aware of ourselves and our place in the world.

This is where current AI falls flat. Today's fanciest AIs are more like talking toasters – they can fake feelings in what they say and do, but there's nobody home inside. Siri can respond with witty banter, but does it have any inner spark, any true sense of self?

From the outside, even the most convincing AI still seems to be just a talented mimic, not a sentient being. It's imitating the surface features of human consciousness and emotion, but there's no ghost in the machine, no genuine inner life.

This brings up some deep philosophical puzzles. How would we even know if an AI was conscious? We can't even agree on which animals are sentient! The problem of figuring out if a machine can be conscious is going to be a hard one.

But I believe that creating AI with genuine self-awareness will be key to achieving human-level intelligence. It's not enough to just process information – it needs some kind of inner experience, some sense of self.

Connection: No AI Is an Island

Last but not least, let's remember that human intelligence is social. It isn't just about our individual brainpower – it's about how we connect with other people, animals, nature, and the whole universe.

Language isn't just a tool for thinking, but for bonding, for sharing ideas and feelings. Same goes for empathy, humor, art, spirituality, ethics – these aren't just add-ons to our intelligence, but the things that give our thoughts shape and direction.

Think about how a child gets smarter by chatting and playing with family and friends. Or how students sharpen their wits by debating and collaborating with classmates. Or how scientists push the frontiers of knowledge by building on the work of their peers.

And our connections go beyond just other humans. Our relationships with animals and nature play a huge role too. Have you ever been jolted awake in the middle of the night by your dog barking? What do you do? Most of us would get up and check to see if something is amiss, right? That's not just blind trust in our furry friends – it's a form of interspecies communication that's been honed over thousands of years of coexistence.

If you're hiking in the woods, for example, and suddenly see a group of animals all fleeing in the same direction. Your instinct tells you there's danger in the direction they're running from, right? That's your intelligence tapping into the collective wisdom of the natural world. This kind of interspecies communication and understanding is a unique aspect of human intelligence that we often take for granted.

And it's not just animals - recent research suggests that plants might be communicating too, in ways we're only beginning to understand. Did you know that stressed plants actually 'cry'? Scientists have discovered that plants make ultrasonic sounds when they're thirsty or injured - up to 35 sounds per hour.[7] We can't hear these sounds because they're too high-pitched for human ears, but some animals probably can. Researchers have even trained AI models to determine whether a plant is water-stressed or damaged just by listening to these sounds.

This discovery opens up a whole new dimension of potential intelligence in the natural world. Are plants 'talking' to each other? Are animals listening? Could this be a form of ecosystem-wide communication we've been oblivious to all this time? It's mind-boggling to think about, and it shows just how much we still have to learn about intelligence in all its forms.

But it's still a far cry from the kind of connection that we feel when we interact with others. Human intelligence thrives in connection and community. For AI to match human intelligence, it needs to do more than just exchange data. It needs to build relationships, to participate in creating shared meaning and understanding. It's not just about what happens in individual brains, but the sparks that fly between them.

Seizing the AI Opportunity

Breaking down intelligence into bite-sized bits, I hope you can see both how far AI has come and how far it still has to go. The AI of today can do some incredible things in narrow domains. It can spot cancers better than doctors, compose music in any style, and beat the world's best poker players. We're living in remarkable times!

But when you compare these systems to the full range of human intelligence, you realize they're still limited. They're incredibly skilled at specific tasks, but without the rich, general understanding that lets humans navigate the world so well.

Things are about to get exciting. The gap between narrow AI and artificial general intelligence presents a huge opportunity for folks like you! Building really robust AI is going to take all hands-on deck, not just the computer scientists and engineers. Your know-how in things like sniffing out fraud, sizing up risks, and keeping things on the level could be the secret ingredient in taking AI to the next level.

By bringing your brainpower to the table – with all its real-world understanding, judgment, and human touch – you can help shape an AI that doesn't just talk a good game, but really gets it.

The future belongs to those who can build bridges between the technical and the ethical, the scientific and the social. By digging into intelligence from all angles, we're laying the groundwork for machines that don't just crunch data, but grasp ideas; that don't just spit out answers but figure out how to ask the right questions.

So, here's my challenge to you: stay curious! Don't be afraid to ponder the big questions of intelligence and consciousness. Keep pushing to understand how these breakthroughs could reshape your work. And above all, bring your full humanity to the table.

8

Rule 3: Today's Reality Defines Current Intelligence and History Defines Current Reality

THE WORLD IS CHANGING so fast it'll make your head spin! Nowhere is this more obvious than with artificial intelligence. Breakthroughs that sounded like science fiction just a few years ago are becoming real as we speak. To wrap our heads around this, we've got to start with a fundamental truth: Reality is always changing, shaped by the constant growth of technology and human understanding.

It's easy to think of AI as something entirely new, totally separate from human history. But today's AI has deep roots in the long story of biological intelligence that came before it. To really understand where artificial intelligence is going, we need to look at how human intelligence emerged and evolved over thousands of years. In short, today's reality defines current intelligence, and history defines current reality.

Remember our time traveler from chapter 1 from 1850? Back then, it took about 6 months to travel from San Francisco to New York by stagecoach or sailing ship. Just 50 years later in 1900 you could make that same journey in 4 days by railroad!

Today, a flight from SF to NY only takes 6 hours. If you told someone from 1900, let alone 1850, that you could cross the country in less time than it takes to get a good night's sleep, they'd think you were nuts!

The point is, at any moment in history, a civilization's "current intelligence" – its cutting-edge intellectual achievements – is defined by the realities and limits of the time. AI is no exception. Today's most advanced AI systems, despite their amazing capabilities, are products of the early 21st century world that created them.

To put this in perspective, let's take a quick tour through what I call the Four Eras of Intelligence:

Era 1: The Rise of Greek Rational Thought (~300 BCE - 1600s CE) Ancient Greek thinkers like Aristotle, Euclid, Hypatia and Plato laid the foundations for modern logic, mathematics, and observational science. They planted the seeds of rational inquiry that drive fields like computer science to this day.

Era 2: The Mathematical and Scientific Revolutions (1600s - 1900s) During the Scientific Revolution, pioneers like Newton, Leibniz, and Pascal cooked up mathematical breakthroughs that would prove critical for AI, from calculus to binary code to early computers. The 1800s brought key insights in algebraic logic, programmable machines, and statistical language analysis.

Era 3: The Dawn of Computing (1930s - 1950s) In the early 20th century, visionaries began to dream of thinking machines. Alan Turing imagined artificial intelligence[1], Grace Hopper pioneered software engineering[2], and Claude Shannon founded information theory[3]. The term "artificial intelligence" was coined in 1956 at the Dartmouth Conference[4].

Era 4: The Internet and Deep Learning Explosions (1960s - Present) As computing power grew exponentially, so did the dreams of AI researchers. The 1990s Internet boom provided the vast datasets needed to train machine learning models. In the 2010s, ImageNet[5], deep learning, and specialized hardware propelled AI to human-level performance on tasks like image and speech recognition. Unprecedented connectivity between datasets has the potential to answer many scientific questions simply by connecting the dots.

The Accelerating Pace of Change

Here's a thought experiment to understand the speed of AI progress. Picture a decade that starts with one major breakthrough, then sees that rate double every year. One breakthrough becomes two, then four, eight, sixteen. By the end of the decade, we've packed over a thousand years' worth of "normal" innovation into just ten! Sound far-fetched? Experts predict the 21st century could see 1000 times the technological progress of the 20th, thanks to the explosive growth of AI and other emerging technologies. The implications are mind-boggling.

Think about Moore's Law[6] – the idea that computing power doubles about every two years. That exponential growth has fueled the rise of PCs, smartphones, the internet and more. But with AI, the curve is bending even more sharply upward as AI systems bootstrap their own growth, optimizing and enhancing themselves at superhuman speed.

We're already seeing mind-blowing demonstrations like AlphaFold cracking 50-year-old protein folding puzzles[7], or Gemini writing human-like text in hundreds of languages. And those headline-grabbers are just the beginning. Underneath, thousands of researchers are racing to apply AI to everything from discovering new drugs to predicting the stock market to building robots.

Navigating the AI Revolution

History has valuable lessons for navigating this accelerating change. Think back to the dawn of electricity when even the most visionary thinkers could barely imagine the coming wave of innovation. The same was true for other game-changing technologies like the telephone, radio, cars, and airplanes. The initial invention set off an avalanche of breakthroughs that reshaped society in profound and unpredictable ways. People could sense the scale of the coming change, but the details remained hazy.

AI is already charting a similar course. Narrow applications like Siri and fraud detection are giving way to large language models, robotic automation, and self-optimizing systems. But the true game-changers – the AI equivalents of radio, television, and computers – still lie ahead. The biggest ways AI will be used are almost certainly ways we haven't even thought about.

Consider green energy as an example. Now, solar energy is cheaper than fossil fuels in most of the world and it is continuing to decline in cost. This could enable massive breakthroughs in fields like desalination[8]. When energy becomes very cheap, processes that were once too costly become viable, opening up entirely new avenues for innovation. Imagine solar power making desalination so affordable that it solves water scarcity issues globally. Just as with AI, we can't predict where the next breakthroughs will come from, but we can be sure they'll reshape our world in ways we can hardly imagine.

So, what can the long history of intelligence tell us about where AI is headed? Here are some key themes:

Change will keep accelerating. AI progress is outpacing even our wildest predictions. Breakthroughs that used to take years are happening in months, and ideas are turning into world-changing inventions practically overnight. Keeping up with AI will demand that you stay connected and always be open to learning new things.

Breakthroughs will come from unexpected places. Many of the biggest AI innovations won't come from tech giants or research labs. They'll come from experts in other fields finding clever ways to apply AI to their work. Some of the biggest innovations will happen where maturing technologies collide, as we're seeing when AI mixes with things like robotics or biotech. As Thomas Kuhn argues in "The Structure of Scientific Revolutions," scientific progress often happens in cycles[9]. Regular, day-to-day science gets disrupted by big paradigm shifts where breakthroughs arise from questioning established norms and blending different disciplines.

Ethical challenges are huge. As AI gets smarter, it will be making big decisions that affect real people's lives in fields like healthcare, finance, and transportation. We need rock-solid frameworks to ensure AI is used safely and ethically. This is where your expertise as CPAs – your commitment to integrity and public trust – will be incredibly valuable.

AI will redefine work itself. AI will shake up a lot of industries and jobs. But it will also create new opportunities that we can't even imagine yet. The key to futureproofing your career? Stay ahead of the curve. Keep learning, keep adapting, and you'll be ready for whatever comes next.

8 | RULE 3: TODAY'S REALITY DEFINES CURRENT INTELLIGENCE

While a lot about how AI will evolve is still unknown, one thing is clear: the only thing we can count on is change. Each new generation will redefine what counts as intelligence. History shows that those who adapt and stay flexible are best positioned to shape AI.

For CPAs navigating this new world, the way forward is clear. Ground yourself in your profession's core values – ethics, accuracy and accountability. Stay curious about the ways AI is changing accounting. Look to history for inspiration on dreaming up new applications. The goal isn't to predict the future, but to build the agility to adapt as AI reshapes reality.

Remember, AI is a tool. A mind-blowingly powerful one, but still a tool. It will be shaped by the humans using it as much as it shapes us in return. As Fei-Fei Li, a pioneer in AI and computer vision, wisely noted: "The promise of machine intelligence is better understanding of the human kind."[10] Her insight reminds us that AI isn't just about creating smart machines, but about deepening our understanding of ourselves and our potential.

CPAs have a unique opportunity to help steer this technology toward making the world a better place. Have the courage to help lead the AI revolution with your blend of numerical smarts and human judgment. Stay rooted in the past, clear-eyed about the present, and optimistic about the future.

9

Rule 4: Before Using AI Tools, CPAs Must Understand their Strengths and Weaknesses

BEFORE WE START TALKING about AI tools, I want to hammer home one crucial point: AI is incredibly powerful, but it's not a magic wand. Just like any other technology, it has its strengths and its limitations. And if you want to harness its full potential (while avoiding any nasty surprises), you've got to understand exactly what those are.

In this chapter, we'll give you a roadmap for navigating the current AI landscape. Our goal isn't to turn you into tech wizards overnight, but to give you a solid understanding of the tools in your AI toolkit and some principles for using them effectively. Armed with this know-how, you'll be ready to separate AI fact from fiction, dream up creative new applications, and make sure the technology develops in a way that serves the greater good.

The Five Pillars of the AI Toolkit

We're going to focus on five main technologies you need to know about:

1. Generative AI and Large Language Models
2. Chatbots
3. Prompt Querying
4. Multimodal Approaches
5. Synthetic Data

The AI landscape changes daily, and today's hot new tool could be old news tomorrow. Instead of obsessing over current gadgets, we are focusing on core concepts that will serve you well no matter what the future brings. Think of it like learning to cook – once you've nailed the basic techniques, you can whip up a killer meal with whatever ingredients you have on hand.

Generative AI: The Language of Machines

Unless you've been living under a rock (or buried in spreadsheets), you've likely heard about the AI systems that

9 | RULE 4: UNDERSTAND AI TOOLS STRENGTHS AND WEAKNESSES

can write novels, paint masterpieces, and code apps from simple text prompts. These large language models (LLMs) are trained on massive amounts of data and can produce some pretty convincing outputs.

For CPAs, the possibilities are exciting, from drafting financial reports to analyzing contracts to automating basic client communications. Tools like Ernst & Young's Document Intelligence platform[1] already harness natural language processing (NLP) to extract key information from complex documents. Imagine being able to feed a bunch of raw financial data into one of these models and have it spit out a beautifully written analysis. As this technology advances, it could take on even more complicated tasks, freeing you up to focus on the big picture.

But generative AI isn't perfect. Sometimes, it can confidently say things that aren't true. And even the folks who built them don't always understand exactly how they arrive at their outputs.

That's why CPAs need to be careful when using generative AI. You will have to learn how to give clear, specific instructions to get the best results. And you can't just take whatever it spits out as truth – you've got to put on your CPA hat and scrutinize it carefully. Are there any red flags or inconsistencies? Does it actually make sense in the context of the client's business? Those are the kinds of questions you will need to ask.

Another big consideration is whether to go with an "open source" or "closed source" model. Open source means the code and training data is public, so there's more transparency into how it works. Closed source models are more of a black box –

you don't really know what's going on under the hood, though the models might be more advanced. There are pros and cons to each approach, and you should weigh them carefully depending on your specific needs.

Like human communication, different models have their own unique "personalities" shaped by their training data and design. Some are focused on raw speed and scale, while others prioritize safety and truthfulness. As the models get more sophisticated, they're even developing distinctive communication styles – almost like regional dialects! Be aware that LLMs can reproduce biases found in their training data, so monitoring for biased or toxic content is a must. And transparency about what's human-written vs. AI-generated will be important for maintaining trust.

Ultimately, the key with generative AI is to start small and be intentional. Pick a well-defined use case, test a lot, and have clear human checkpoints along the way to validate the outputs. Don't just turn it loose and hope for the best!

Chatbots: Your New Digital Coworker

Chatbots are the friendly face of AI. They can engage in back-and-forth conversations, handling all sorts of customer questions and tasks. And as they get smarter, they'll be able to take on more complicated jobs.

Imagine being able to offload all those routine questions and requests that eat up so much of your time – things like "Can I deduct this expense?" or "When are my taxes due?" With a well-designed chatbot, you could automate those conversations and free yourself up to focus on higher-value work.

But again, it's not just a matter of flipping a switch and letting the chatbot handle everything. Chatbots are only as good as the information they're given and keeping their knowledge up to date takes work. You've got to keep a close eye on the outputs to make sure they're accurate and appropriate. And since they deal with sensitive financial data, security is a top concern. You will need strong safeguards to protect against hacks and data breaches.

One of the coolest things about modern chatbots is that they learn from each interaction so they will give better and better service over time. It's almost like having a tireless, infinitely patient assistant that gets smarter every day.

Multimodal: Flexing All Your Senses

While language is a pillar of human intelligence, it's far from the only one. We also learn from images, videos, audio, and interactive experiences. Increasingly, AI systems are expanding to handle all those different data types and draw insights across them. As more of the world's knowledge is written in multimedia formats, multimodal AI fluency will be a must-have asset.

Imagine being able to feed a pile of scanned purchase orders, invoices, and receipts into an AI and have it not just digitize them, but actually analyze them for patterns and anomalies. Or being able to use natural language to ask a question about a financial statement and have the AI generate a visualization of the key trends and ratios – how cool would that be?

But multimodal AI also presents new risks. Deepfakes and synthetic media could blur the line between fact and fiction. How do we balance the benefits with the risks of fabricated evidence? Once again, CPAs' hard-earned reputation for objectivity and rigor will be key to establishing trust in an era where seeing is not always believing.

The possibilities here are endless, and I think they're going to fundamentally change the way CPAs interact with financial data. But again, it's not just about the flashy demos, it's about really understanding what the technology is capable of and how to harness it in a way that serves your clients' needs.

Prompt Engineering: Questions are the new Commands

Next up is prompt engineering, which is just a fancy way of saying "how to ask AI the right questions to get the answers you need."

This is something I'm passionate about, because I think it's one of the most underrated skills in working with AI. So many folks just fire off a basic query and take whatever the machine spits back. But if you don't ask the right question, how can you get the right answer? There's a quote often attributed to Einstein that says if he had an hour to solve a problem, he'd spend the first 55 minutes trying to figure out the question and the last five minutes looking for the solution![2]

9 | RULE 4: UNDERSTAND AI TOOLS STRENGTHS AND WEAKNESSES

Prompting is equal parts art and science. You've got to combine your knowledge with an understanding of how the AI model thinks and processes information. You need to be specific and clear in what you're asking for, and don't forget to build in checkpoints and guardrails to keep the AI on track.

In a way, it's not so different from the kind of probing questions and critical thinking CPAs already excel at. Whether you're grilling a client about their financial statements or quizzing an AI about tax strategies, the key is to frame your prompts in a way that surfaces the information you need.

Some of my favorite prompt engineering techniques come from time-tested approaches like Socratic questioning, legal depositions, and investigative journalism. The common thread is a focus on precision, follow ups, and trying to anticipate how a query could be misinterpreted. Don't leave any wiggle room for the AI to squirm out of giving you the info you're after!

Anthropic, the AI startup behind Claude, has a great framework they call "constitutional AI"[3] – basically a set of ground rules embedded in the AI's base prompt to keep it honest and on-task. I think CPAs could pioneer something similar for accounting inquiries – a kind of "Generally Accepted AI Auditing Principles" baked into every prompt.

Other useful prompting principles:

- Precision is power: The more precise and detailed your prompt, the more on-target the output. Don't just ask for "financial analysis" – spell out the exact metrics, time frames, and comparison points.

- Connect the dots: AI models are incredibly literal-minded. They'll respond to exactly what you ask for, but no more. Providing clear context upfront – the why behind the what – can steer the model toward more useful results.

- Trial and fine-tune: Rarely will you nail the perfect prompt on the first try. Prompting is an iterative dance – generate, evaluate, tweak, repeat. The best results come from patient tinkering.

- Constraints are key: If not guided, AI models can generate outputs that are meandering, contradictory, or biased. Specify the length, style, structure, and factual parameters to help keep the AI on track.

For CPAs, mastering the art of the prompt isn't just about getting better results from AI tools – it's about rethinking how we get information. In a world full of data, the most valuable skill isn't just knowing where to look but knowing what to ask. By crafting prompts that are clear, nuanced, and specific, CPAs can cut through the clutter and turn up the insights that matter most.

9 | RULE 4: UNDERSTAND AI TOOLS STRENGTHS AND WEAKNESSES

Basic Prompt Cheat Sheet:
Act as a [ROLE] perform [TASK] as [FORMAT]

ROLE	TASK
Act as a tech consultant advising a startup...	Outline the key steps for...
You're a historian...	Summarize the pros and cons of...
Act as an AI ethics professor...	Draft a business proposal for...
Play the role of an auditor...	Create a case study on...
Be a marketing expert...	Write a script for a podcast on...
You are a forensic accountant...	Identify challenges in...
	Create a guide for...

FORMAT		OTHER CONTEXT
Bullet points	Markdown	Audience: Explain to a 10 year old, for finance professionals, small business owners, retirees, dad joke fans
Checklist	News article	
Flow chart	Outline	Goal: Enhance customer satisfaction, reduce errors, increase efficiency
FAQ page	Script dialogue	
Formal report	Slideshow	Time frame: Focus on trends in 2024, developments in the last decade, future impact in the next 5 years
Haiku	Summary	
HTML code	Table	Writing style: Academic, conversational, humorous, motivational, persuasive
Infographic	Word cloud	

Synthetic Data: When Fake Beats Real

Finally, we've got synthetic data. I know this one might sound a bit science fiction-y, but it's actually a really clever way to lessen some of the challenges of working with sensitive financial information.

The basic idea is that instead of using real client data to train and test AI models (which can be a privacy and security nightmare), you use generated data that mimics the patterns and statistics of the real thing. That way, you can build and test powerful AI tools without putting any actual client information at risk.

If you're still scratching your head as to why we'd want to swap real data for fake, a cautionary story might help. Back in 2016, I found myself sitting next to a noticeably upset passenger on a post-election flight. He introduced himself as an exec from the infamous Cambridge Analytica firm[4], fresh off a disastrous board meeting with Facebook.

His sad tale revolved around Cambridge Analytica's use of hyper-targeted voter profiles built with personal data from Facebook quizzes and page likes. He grumbled that Facebook blamed them for the model's success in identifying persuadable voters using the 'Big Five' personality traits. He predicted old-school polling would soon die out as data scientists reverse-engineered political and commercial preferences from digital traces.

Fast forward a few years, and his prophecy is mostly fulfilled. Detailed personal profiles now drive the predictive power and hyper-personalization of modern AI. But it has also sparked a massive privacy backlash, scaring users away from sharing their data. Enter synthetic data: algorithmically generated realistic but fake datasets that let organizations use AI without violating strict data regulations.

As a CPA, you need to be aware of this trend. Data privacy regulations are evolving, and synthetic data is becoming increasingly important. And it's not just a defensive play. Synthetic data can also be a powerful tool for modeling and testing out different scenarios and strategies in a risk-free environment.

Imagine being able to generate thousands of realistic financial statements with just a few clicks, and then use AI to stress-test them under different economic conditions or tax regimes. That's the kind of superpower that synthetic data can give you!

But of course, with great power comes great responsibility. As CPAs, it's your job to make sure that any synthetic data you're using is truly representative and unbiased, and that you're not making decisions based on faulty assumptions or flawed models.

Navigating the AI Frontier

So, there you have it. The five key tools that every CPA needs to understand in the AI age! The main thing I want you to take away is this: AI is not something to be feared or ignored – it's an incredible opportunity to take your practice to the next level and deliver even more value for your clients.

But it's not a magic bullet, and it's not something you can just "set and forget." To really harness the power of AI, you've got to roll up your sleeves and put in the work to understand how it ticks, what it's capable of, and where its limits lie. And you've got to approach it with the same rigor, skepticism, and commitment to ethics that have always been the hallmark of the CPA profession.

If you can do that, I have no doubt that you'll be able to ride the wave of AI disruption and come out on top. Because at the end of the day, the real value of a CPA isn't just in crunching numbers or filling out forms – it's in the judgment, insight, and integrity you bring to every engagement. And no machine can ever replace that.

10

Rule 5: New Tools for CPAs in the Age of AI

RULE 5 MIGHT SEEM a bit out there at first. We're not just talking about the AI tools you already know like chatbots, prompt querying, or multimodal interfaces. In this chapter we will be getting into the cutting-edge stuff that's about to revolutionize your work.

My goal is to arm you with a basic understanding of artificial intelligence so you can hold your own in conversations with experts. The previous chapter covered the tools currently in use. Now, we're taking things a step further. In this chapter we will be exploring those AI tools that you could be using soon that will help you unlock your Super AI CPA powers.

The Future is Already Here

Whenever I talk about advancements in technology, science or civilization, I always think of that William Gibson quote mentioned in chapter 2: "The future is already here – it's just not evenly distributed." Take driverless cars for example. Autonomous taxis are already zipping around the streets of Singapore and San Francisco. The driverless future has arrived; it just hasn't hit every street corner... yet.

The same goes for these new AI tools. They're out there, waiting for smart CPAs like you to grab them and run. And the ones who do are going to have a serious leg up on the competition.

So, what are these new tools? In essence, they are seven game-changing ways AI is about to supercharge your Super AI CPA powers.

Seven New Ways to Leverage AI Processes

1. Using Text and Images Along with Numbers

Gone are the days when CPAs only dealt with numbers. AI is bringing text and images into the mix, and it is opening up a whole new world of possibilities. AI can extract data from things like contracts, invoices, and expense reports. It can even get insights from images like receipts and shipping labels.

Imagine an AI-powered balance sheet that doesn't just show numbers but visualizes your company's financial health. Picture cash as a pie chart, receivables as a colorful timeline, and liabilities as a heat map. Suddenly, financial data becomes a lot more understandable for everyone, not just the number-crunchers.

But it goes beyond pretty pictures. AI can extract data from emails, receipts, and even surveillance footage. Think about what that means for fraud detection. An AI system could spot discrepancies that would slip right past a traditional audit. Of course, it's up to the CPA to make sure these powerful tools are used responsibly.

2. Applying Mathematical Principles to Text and Images

Algebra, geometry, calculus – AI is taking those principles and applying them to text and images, unlocking powerful new applications for CPAs.

Picture this: You're PepsiCo with a fleet of 22,000 Frito-Lay delivery trucks. You snap photos at the start of each day, and at every stop. Then at the end of the day, you take a final picture of what's left in the truck.

With AI, you can analyze those images using algebraic equations. By comparing the before and after photos, AI can flag any trucks with discrepancies without any manual counting!

Or think about audits. AI could analyze the language patterns in emails, meeting minutes, and even earnings call transcripts to sniff out potential fraud or disclosure issues. It's like doing a linguistic audit alongside a financial audit!

3. Allowing AI to Learn and Suggest Improvements

Now we are entering a realm where AI doesn't just follow orders but comes up with ideas of its own. These AI systems can spot inefficiencies and suggest improvements based on the data they process.

Let's take a look at a few examples, starting with our Frito-Lay delivery routes. An AI looking at the truck fleet data might propose a way to minimize traffic lights and reduce the average route time. Just as Google Maps suggests alternate routes based on real-time traffic, AI could optimize operations by learning and offering improvements.

An AI accounts payable system might notice that vendors are submitting invoices late and suggest changing contract terms to speed up payment cycles. An AI financial planning tool might notice that a client's spending is out of sync with their stated goals and suggest a budget adjustment. These kinds of AI systems are like having a super-smart assistant constantly learning and looking for ways to improve operations.

The key is to give AI some room to think outside the box. Ask it open-ended questions and see what it comes up with. CPAs who do this will be amazed at the insights AI can uncover.

4. Asking the Right Questions

I can't stress enough how important it is to craft effective prompts and ask good questions. This is a critical skill in the age of AI. The art of "prompt engineering" might even be more important than the technical aspects of AI systems themselves.

For example, instead of asking "What's our cash conversion cycle?" try "Based on our five-year financial history, what changes to our credit policy would optimize working capital while keeping customers happy?" See the difference?

As a Super AI CPA, you need to think of AI as a collaborator, not just a calculator. That's why learning to craft thoughtful, detailed prompts is so important. Those kinds of prompts will give you much more valuable answers.

5. Incorporating AI Across All Business Functions

AI isn't just for the accounting or IT departments. It should be woven throughout the entire organization, supporting decision-making across all functions.

An AI risk management system, for example, could feed a real-time "credit score" to the sales team's CRM, allowing them to adjust deal terms for at-risk clients. An AI-powered demand forecast could help manufacturing optimize production. A predictive HR model could even help retention efforts for critical roles.

The CFO of the future won't just be a number-cruncher, but a strategic partner driving insights across the entire organization.

6. AI Learning Autonomously - with Human Guidance

Here's where things get both exciting and a little scary. AI systems are starting to learn and adapt on their own, without explicit programming. It's powerful stuff, but it needs careful oversight.

For example, an AI auditing tool could be great at spotting fraud patterns in an expense report database. Maybe it finds that employees whose first names start with "J" are slightly more likely to fudge their mileage reimbursements. Could it then decide to flag all J-names for extra scrutiny? Maybe, but that's exactly the kind of bias CPAs need to spot and correct for.

Or what about an AI tax optimizer that gets a little too creative in exploiting loopholes? When does "tax avoidance" cross the line into tax evasion? These matters of professional judgment can't be entirely turned over to algorithms, no matter how sophisticated.

The next wave of AI accounting tools will need to have what researchers call "constitutional constraints" – ethical principles, decision boundaries, and human oversight – baked into the models. CPAs have a vital role in keeping these systems in check.

7. The Need for Ethical Regulations and Guardrails

As AI grows more sophisticated, we need to make sure it's not just smart, but also wise. As these systems become more powerful and pervasive, we need to ensure they're aligned with human values.

This can't be left to the tech companies. As trusted advisors with deep understanding of financial systems, CPAs have a vital role to play in shaping AI ethics. Ask the hard questions: How do we audit AI for bias? What oversight is needed as algorithms impact markets and economies?

This is your chance to imbue AI with the ethical foundations that have long been the hallmark of the CPA profession.

Competitive Advantages for CPAs

Now that we've explained the seven game-changing ways that new AI tools will impact accounting, it's time to talk about how CPAs can use these new tools to gain a competitive advantage.

AI-powered tools will create opportunities for Super AI CPAs to gain an edge. Here are some concrete examples of how you can leverage these new tools:

Algebraic Thinking Applied to Assets, Liabilities and Equity

While CPAs have traditionally used the asset = liabilities + owner's equity equation to analyze financial statements, AI enables extending this algebraic thinking to whole new domains.

Imagine evaluating potential hires or acquisitions using an AI that quantifies skills and experience as "assets" and "liabilities." This kind of AI tool will allow you to extend financial frameworks into new domains. The CPA of the future will use AI to surface unexpected algebraic insights from data of all types.

Truth Verification Across Various Inputs

CPAs will not just be auditing numbers anymore. AI lets you cross-reference and verify data across documents, databases, and even verbal statements. With AI it will be like having superpowered lie-detector glasses for financial data.

Imagine an AI that can automatically reconcile a CEO's verbal earnings guidance against the notes in the 10K/10Q – or even against the metadata in an Outlook calendar. Or an AI that can instantly sniff out invoice fraud by spotting discrepancies in the placement of logos and signatures in a pdf. As they say, "trust but verify" – supercharged with AI's pattern-matching ability.

Improving Tax Policy Compliance and Efficiency

AI-powered tools are a game changer, capable of tracking ever-changing tax laws across jurisdictions, ensuring compliance while optimizing for every allowable benefit. This can help both filers and authorities make sense of it all!

Intelligent agents can automatically flag high-risk tax positions and recommend strategies to minimize audit exposure. On the government side, AI could make audits far more targeted and less burdensome by finding likely cases of evasion/avoidance. And over time, analysis of filing patterns and problems could improve the tax code itself – simplifying rules, streamlining forms, and easing compliance in ways humans writing the laws might not think of. The future of tax planning and preparation can be proactive, with AI-augmented counsel leading the way, instead of reactive and clean-up.

Predicting Performance Through Non-Linear Analogies

In the age of AI, CPAs can go beyond reporting financial performance to predicting it. AI excels at forecasting by spotting patterns. By training AI on years of historical financial statements and economic data, CPAs can create financial projections with unheard of accuracy. You'll be able to advise clients not just on past performance, but on how to navigate the future with confidence.

As a Super AI CPA, your role is to combine the technical power of these predictive models with the strategic wisdom to help clients act on them. AI-powered predictions are becoming essential for navigating an uncertain future, and CPAs who harness that tool will be the most trusted navigators in the challenging times ahead.

Supply Chain Alerts

Remember the great toilet paper shortage of 2020? Shortages of goods like computer chips and baby formula seemed to catch companies and policymakers off guard. In reality, the warning signs were there in the data – for those able to interpret it.

With AI monitoring supply chains 24/7, CPAs can provide their clients with an early warning system for disruptions that let businesses get ahead of crises.

Analysis of Mistakes

AI can sift through mountains of transactions to flag potential errors or fraud faster than any human could. More importantly, it can learn over time to distinguish innocent mistakes from suspected fraud. Using AI is like having a tireless, eagle-eyed audit team working for you around the clock.

Rooting out accounting errors will always require a human touch, but AI can shine a light on where to look.

Shape the AI Future - or Be Shaped by It

The rise of AI isn't some far-off sci-fi fantasy. It's here, it's real, and it needs CPAs like you to help chart its course. The CPAs who embrace these tools – who learn to use them responsibly and creatively – are going to be the superstars of tomorrow.

Most exciting of all, is the chance for CPAs to be the moral compass in this brave new world. Who better to make sure these powerful tools stay honest and ethical?

Your job isn't to become a coder or an AI engineer. It's to be the bridge between cutting-edge technology and time-honored professional judgment. By asking the right questions, demanding transparency, and keeping a watchful eye out for any funny business, you'll be the guardians making sure AI plays by the rules and serves the public good.

The CPAs who dive in, experiment, and pioneer new applications of AI will be the rock stars of accounting. You'll be the secret weapon for businesses navigating this data-rich, AI-powered landscape. You'll be building new forms of assurance for the algorithmic age. You'll be spotting risks and opportunities that even the tech experts might miss.

In short, you'll be a Super AI CPA, capable of using incredible technological power while staying true to human values and wisdom. Remember, no matter how impressive artificial intelligence is, it is still artificial. It needs your real, human expertise to guide it.

11

Rule 6: The Quest for AI Consciousness

For AI to Create Consciousness, It Must Experience Pleasure, Pain, and be able to Define Wisdom Without Mortality.

Consciousness is one of the most mind-bending topics in AI. What does it mean for AI to be "conscious?" Is it even possible? How can we enable AI to experience the essential elements of consciousness?

The Consciousness Conundrum

Let's start with an even simpler question (if you paid attention to Rule 2 you know where I'm going with this): What exactly is consciousness? If you're hoping for a nice, neat scientific definition, I've got some bad news for you – there isn't one. Even the brightest minds in neuroscience, philosophy, and AI research are still debating this one. Even with all our fancy brain scans and philosophical debates, we still can't quite pin down what makes us... well, us.

But don't worry. Just because we can't nail down a precise definition doesn't mean we're totally in the dark. When we think about consciousness, we talk about things like having a sense of humor, the ability to feel pleasure and pain, emotional experience, the passage of time and mortality. These are all aspects of the human experience that contribute to our understanding of what it means to be conscious.

Now, before you start wondering if this chapter accidentally got swapped with a philosophy textbook, let me assure you, understanding consciousness is essential as we navigate the brave new world of AI. Why? Because if we want AI to truly reach human-level intelligence, it needs to develop its own form of consciousness. And that, my friends, is where things get really interesting.

The Three Flavors of Consciousness

To make things a bit more manageable, let's break consciousness down into three types:

1. **Primary Consciousness:** This is the basic "I exist" level. It's about survival instincts - eating, sleeping, breathing. It's what a mouse has when it scurries away from a cat. For AI, this would be the ability to process inputs and respond to its environment.

2. **Binary Consciousness:** Think of this as the "us vs. them" mentality. It's what drives sports rivalries, political debates, and competitive analysis. For AI, this could be recognizing itself as distinct from other systems or users.

3. **Higher-Level Consciousness:** This is about collective awareness, empathy, and those moments of profound connection to the universe. It's what makes a firefighter rush into a burning building to save a stranger, or what inspires an artist to create a masterpiece that moves people to tears. For AI, this would include complex reasoning, ethical decision-making, and possibly even self-reflection.

Why does this matter for CPAs and financial professionals? Well, think about the decisions you must make in your work. Those choices often require a blend of all three levels of consciousness: basic survival instincts (protecting yourself and your clients), competitive thinking (navigating market forces), and higher-level considerations (upholding ethical standards for the greater good). As we build more advanced AI systems to assist in financial decision-making, we need to think about how they will navigate these complex waters

The Ingredients of Consciousness

Creating artificial consciousness isn't like following a recipe. You can't just throw some algorithms in a pot, stir in some data, and voila! Conscious AI. But there are some key ingredients we can identify:

Observations: This is the raw data of consciousness. What we see, hear, smell, taste, and touch shape our conscious experience. AI can already process huge amounts of sensory data, but an AI system needs to "see" the world from multiple perspectives to develop a richer understanding.

Cultural Values: Our upbringing and cultural background shape how we interpret our observations. It's not just about programming rules – it's about understanding context and nuance. If you grew up in a culture where eating pork is taboo, your conscious experience of bacon will be very different from someone raised on BLTs.

Philosophical Questions: These are the big, unanswerable questions that keep philosophy professors employed. "What is the meaning of life?" "Is there a God?" "Is a hot dog a sandwich?" AI needs to tackle these abstract concepts, not just to find answers, but to understand why we ask these questions in the first place.

Mathematics: Some argue that math is the language of the universe. If it's a human invention, as others say, then AI might develop its own mathematical language to describe consciousness. But if mathematics is the language of the universe, then AI might discover consciousness the same way we did – by observing and understanding the world around it.

The Essential Experiences

But developing consciousness isn't just about processing information. It's about experiencing the world in all its messy glory. And that brings us to some essential elements of consciousness that AI will need to grapple with.

First up: pleasure. AI can tell you the best pizza joint in town, but can it savor that perfect bite? Can it experience the joy of a sunset or the thrill of a rollercoaster? This is more than just a philosophical question. In the business world, understanding pleasure drives consumer behavior, influences decision-making, and shapes market trends.

On the flip side, we've got pain and struggle. We often think of pain as something to avoid, but it's needed for growth and learning. Can AI understand the concept of "no pain, no gain?" Can it push through discomfort to achieve a goal? Without experiencing pain, how can AI really understand risk or sacrifice?

Then there's the big one: love and romance. Can an AI understand the complex, often irrational nature of human relationships? Can it ever experience the butterflies of a first date or the comfort of a long-term partnership? Or understand why a song can bring tears to our eyes? How can we program an AI to understand why certain behaviors might be annoying from one person but endearing from someone we love?

As CPAs, you know all about trust. Your entire profession is built on it. But trust requires vulnerability, the willingness to open oneself up to potential harm. How do we instill that in a machine?

Now, let's tackle a big one: wisdom versus intelligence. We've been calling it "artificial intelligence" all this time, but maybe we should be aiming for "artificial wisdom." It's the difference between knowing facts and understanding their implications. Wisdom is about understanding context, making judgments, and applying knowledge ethically. Can AI develop the kind of wisdom that comes from years of experience and reflection?

Last, but not least, we've got to talk about rest. Even God took a day off, according to some beliefs. Humans need rest to process information, make decisions, and maintain mental health. But in a system that runs 24/7, how do we replicate the benefits of downtime?

The Tides of the Mind: A Biological Perspective

There's a great book called "The Tides of Mind" by Yale professor David Gelernter[1] that argues consciousness isn't static. Imagine your mind as an ocean. Sometimes it's calm and rational, like when you're deep in concentration. Other times, it's a stormy sea of emotions. These mental "tides" ebb and flow throughout the day, week, or year, influencing our decisions and perceptions. Think about how different you feel first thing in the morning compared to late at night when you're exhausted. Or how your decision-making changes when you're stressed versus when you're calm. Our consciousness is tied to our biological rhythms and processes.

AI, on the other hand, is always "on." It doesn't have those natural rhythms that characterize human consciousness. This book suggests that until AI can mimic this ebb and flow, it will never achieve human-like consciousness. To truly achieve human-like intelligence, AI might need to become more... unstable? It's a wild thought, isn't it?

Tools for Developing AI Consciousness

So, how do we even begin to approach creating consciousness in AI? Well, my friends, it starts with asking the big, dumb questions. You know, the kind of questions a kid might ask that make you stop and go "Huh, I never thought about it that way." These seemingly simple questions often lead to the biggest breakthroughs.

Take medical science, for instance. A big, dumb question there was, "How can we turn the immune system on and off like a switch?" That simple question led to mapping the human genome and now we have thousands of potential approaches to curing diseases by flipping cellular switches. Pretty amazing, right? We need to approach AI development with this kind of open, curious mindset.

We also need new ways to test for consciousness. The old Turing test[2] just doesn't cut it anymore. One idea comes from an MIT professor who suggests a test based on financial creativity. If an AI can come up with multiple ways to turn $100,000 into a million dollars within a month, it will have achieved a form of consciousness[3]. Now, I'm not saying this is the be-all and end-all of consciousness tests, but it's an interesting approach to measuring adaptability and creative problem-solving.

Here's a fun one for you: Fermi's Paradox[4]. Enrico Fermi, a brilliant physicist, once asked, "If there are so many habitable planets out there, why haven't we heard from any other civilizations?" One theory is the "Great Filter"[5] – a hurdle that civilizations must overcome to survive long-term. Some think that developing AI could be our Great Filter. If we create superintelligent AI, will it help us break through to a new level of existence, or will it be our downfall? Heavy stuff, I know.

CPAs are all about spotting patterns and applying knowledge across different domains. But sometimes, the best way to do that is to think laterally -- take a solution from one area and apply it to another. For example, use risk assessment techniques from auditing to evaluate investment opportunities. In AI research, it could mean applying ideas from fields like biology, psychology, or even art to develop new approaches. This kind of creative problem-solving is essential for developing AI consciousness.

And finally, we have the application of Bayes' theorem[6] to common sense reasoning. Yejin Choi, the Wissner-Slivka Chair of Computer Science at the University of Washington, is using this statistical approach to help AI systems develop intuition and make more human-like decisions – you know, all those little things we take for granted but are incredibly hard to program into a computer. It's like how you develop a "gut feel" for detecting financial irregularities after years of experience.

The CPA's Role in Developing AI Consciousness

So, how can you, as future Super AI CPAs, contribute to the development of AI consciousness? Well, it all comes back to what you do best: trust and verification. You are experts at sniffing out inconsistencies, spotting patterns, and applying rigorous standards to complex systems. These are exactly the skills needed to develop and evaluate AI consciousness.

You could apply your fraud detection skills to helping AI systems catch fake answers. You are trained to spot anomalies, to question when things don't add up. These skills would be invaluable in developing AI systems that can call out wrong or misleading information, or in creating an AI tool that can explain its decision-making process in a way that's transparent and verifiable.

Imagine a world where AI systems come with a "CPA Seal of Approval." It wouldn't just be about verifying the accuracy of the system's outputs, but also about ensuring the ethical use of data, the fairness of decision-making processes, and the overall trustworthiness of the AI system.

The Road Ahead

Creating artificial consciousness is not just a technical challenge – it's also a philosophical and ethical one. We're not just building machines; we're potentially creating new forms of intelligence that could reshape our world in profound ways.

Remember, the goal isn't to replicate human consciousness exactly, but to develop AI systems that can operate with a level of awareness and ethical understanding that we associate with consciousness.

As we continue to push the boundaries of AI, we need to keep asking the big questions. Can an AI system truly experience pleasure and pain? Can it develop wisdom without mortality? How do we measure and verify consciousness?

But is human-like consciousness even the right goal for AI? Or should we be aiming for something entirely different – a form of machine consciousness that's distinct from, but complementary to, human consciousness?

As CPAs, you bring a valuable perspective to this challenge. Your skills in analysis, verification, and ethical decision-making are exactly what's needed in the development of responsible AI. Don't underestimate the impact you can have in this field. You might not have all the answers, but you certainly know how to ask the right questions and verify the results.

Remember, in the world of AI consciousness, we're all still students. Stay curious. Keep asking those "dumb" questions, and never stop learning. After all, isn't that what consciousness is all about?

12

Rule 7: Ethical Foundations for Super AI CPAs

WELCOME TO OUR FINAL RULE, and it's a big one: AI tools will create both good and bad Super AI CPA outcomes. That's why ethics and guardrails must be established.

The Rise of the Super AI CPA

When I first started talking about Super AI CPAs, I'll admit, I felt a bit silly. It sounds like something out of a comic book, right? But the more I've thought and worked with this, the more I've realized how spot-on it really is. We're not just talking about CPAs using AI as a fancy calculator. We're talking about a whole new breed of accountant – one that combines human smarts with AI superpowers.

Think about it this way: It was a big step when humans stopped walking everywhere and began harnessing animals, like horses, for transportation. But humans working with machines (like cars and jets) was a whole new ballgame. It's the same with AI. A human CPA is great. An AI working alone can do some cool tricks. But a human CPA partnering with AI? That's going to be mind-blowing.

The age of AI is here, and a truly "super" AI CPA may be just around the corner. Mark my words: In the not-too-distant future, being a Super AI CPA won't just be a competitive advantage. It will be necessary to stay in the game. Those who don't adapt might find themselves going the way of the abacus. Harsh, I know, but that's the reality we're facing.

But this incredible power comes with equally incredible responsibility. A Super AI CPA understands the ins and outs of artificial intelligence – not just how to use it, but why it works the way it does. What it's good at and where it falls short. A Super AI CPA will need to be able to look at an AI system and see not just what it can do, but what it might do if pushed in the wrong direction.

How many times have I stressed the trust and verification point in this book? Well, get ready to hear it again, because it's essential when it comes to AI development. We need CPAs to bring their honest, skeptical minds to the AI tools themselves.

The Three Parts of AI Ethics

There are three key parts to consider when it comes to the ethics of AI:

1. Individual, Family, and Environmental Ethics
2. Group Standards, Oaths, and Missions
3. Societal Rules and Government Regulations

Individual, Family, and Environmental Ethics

This first part is the moral compass we develop through our personal experiences, upbringing, and surroundings. We're talking about those core values that often reveal themselves in times of crisis.

Think about it – the values instilled in you by your parents, the lessons learned through triumphs and mistakes, the norms of the community you grew up in – all of them shape your approach to ethical questions. And AI is going to present us with some big dilemmas!

Consider this classic ethical puzzle: You're on a sinking boat with only two other people – your mother and a brilliant scientist who's about to cure cancer. You can only save one of them. Who do you choose?

If you pick your mom, you might be what ethicists call a "formalist" – someone who believes in absolute moral rules, like "always protect your family." If you choose the scientist, you're more of a "rationalist," which is someone who tries to do the most good for the most people. There's no objectively "right" answer to this conundrum, but how you approach it says a lot about your ethical framework.

Now, let's put this in accounting terms. Imagine an AI system that can catch fraud like nobody's business, but it digs into people's personal lives to do it. Is the benefit to society worth giving up privacy? These are the kinds of thorny issues Super AI CPAs will face.

Group Standards, Oaths, and Missions

The second part deals with professional ethical standards. These are the formal codes of conduct, the oaths we take, and the stated missions of the institutions we're part of. CPAs have a well-established ethical code that emphasizes integrity, objectivity, competence, and confidentiality. But how do these time-honored principles translate to an AI-powered world?

Take confidentiality. It used to mean locking file cabinets and password-protecting computers. But with AI systems that can connect dots across separate data sources, what will true confidentiality look like? How do we keep AI from spilling secrets by accident?

Or what about professional competence? As AI gets smarter, it's tempting to lean on it too much. How can you keep your skills sharp while using AI? Where's the line between getting a helpful boost and just outsourcing your job to a machine?

These are the kinds of questions we need to be asking as we develop ethical frameworks for AI. We need to look at our professional oaths and standards with fresh eyes and figure out how they apply in this new world of AI.

Societal Rules and Government Regulations

The third part covers the big picture stuff – the rules and regulations that govern society as a whole. This is really interesting right now, because AI is moving much faster than the law. We're in a Wild West situation with AI. There's a lot of talk about how to control it. But real laws and rules are just starting to show up.

This puts a lot of responsibility on individual professions and organizations to create their own rules and best practices for now. For CPAs, this is both a challenge and an opportunity. You can help shape these new regulations, pushing for guidelines that protect the public good and still let innovation thrive. But it also means being very careful right now, creating your own guardrails while waiting for the law to catch up.

So, should AI guardrails be loose or tight? I don't think it's a one-size-fits-all answer. In areas where lives are at stake – military or healthcare – we need those guardrails to be pretty tight. But in more creative or low-stakes fields, like music or art? We can probably loosen things up a bit.

This is where a Super AI CPA comes in. We need you to help write the rulebook for AI in finance. If we leave it all up to the computer science folks and the tech companies, we might end up with a financial system that's clever but ethically bankrupt. People trust financial statements because CPAs hold them to high standards. We need to bring that same integrity to the world of AI.

The Ethical Adventures of a Super AI CPA

Being a Super AI CPA isn't just about using cool new tools. It's about understanding the ethical implications of those tools and using them responsibly. It's about looking at an AI-generated financial report and not just checking that the numbers add up, but also asking deeper questions. Is this fair? Is it clear? Is this serving the public good?

Remember that sinking boat problem? Being a Super AI CPA means facing ethical questions like that all the time. You might have to choose between using an AI tool that could boost profits and one that's more transparent but less lucrative. You'll need to balance short-term gains against long-term risks, not just for your clients, but for the integrity of the whole financial system.

But it's not all doom and gloom! Being a Super AI CPA also means having incredible tools at your fingertips. Imagine analyzing mountains of financial data in seconds. Picture spotting patterns that would take a person months to find. Think about running thousands of "what-if" scenarios, helping your clients make smarter decisions. That's the kind of value a Super AI CPA can bring to the table.

Some of you might be feeling a bit overwhelmed and wondering, "Am I cut out to be a Super AI CPA? Do I have what it takes?" Well, let's go back to our time-travel story about the early days of electricity. Imagine you're living at the turn of the last century. A friend rushes in shouting "I just saw that electrical stuff and there was a wire of it in water and I was just about to walk through it and my friend walked through it and he's dead!" Woah. But then another friend comes in and says, "Hey, guess what? Thanks to that electrical thing, I stayed up all last night writing and I wrote this great new song!"

Which one are you going to be when it comes to AI? The worried skeptic, always looking for danger? Or the excited optimist, eager to explore the possibilities of this new technology? There's no right answer – both views have value. The key is to find a balance – to be excited about the potential of AI while keeping your eyes open for the risks.

The Future is Bright (If We Get This Right)

I want to close with some bold predictions about where all this is heading. I don't have a crystal ball, but I believe we're on the edge of some transformative changes in the world of accounting and AI.

First off, I believe that within the next two to five years, everyone who's read this book will be using some kind of AI in their daily lives. It might be part of your car, your phone, or some gadget we haven't even imagined yet.

Second, I'm willing to bet that we will see a CPA, or a CPA-led company, create an AI tool worth over a billion dollars. That's right, with a "B." Why? Because the skills that make CPAs great – financial analysis, trust, and verification – are going to be absolutely crucial in developing responsible AI systems.

Lastly, I think we're going to see some clever entrepreneur out there start an AI company that hits a billion-dollar valuation with a team of ten people or less. The potential for innovation in this space is just that huge.

The Ethical Imperative

Here's the bottom line: really understanding AI and staying up to date with new developments is going to give you a massive competitive advantage in the years to come. It's not about knowing which buttons to push. It's about understanding the fundamental concepts, seeing the ethical implications, and helping shape where AI goes next.

These AI systems are going to be making big decisions with real-world impact, and we need to think long and hard about the ethics we're baking into them. Remember, AI is a tool. An incredibly powerful tool, but still a tool. It's going to be shaped by the humans using it just as much as it shapes us in return. As CPAs, you have a unique opportunity – even a responsibility – to help steer this technology in a direction that makes the world a better place.

You have a choice to make. You can approach AI with fear and skepticism, always looking for the danger. Or you can embrace it with enthusiasm and creativity, while keeping your eyes open to the challenges. I hope you'll choose the second path. Don't just use AI, shape it. Set the ethical standards. Build the guardrails. Show the world what it truly means to be a Super AI CPA.

The future of accounting isn't just about crunching numbers faster or automating paperwork. It's about using AI to provide deeper insights, make better decisions, and create more value for clients and society. But we need a new kind of accountant to make it happen. The Super AI CPA will harness the power of AI while upholding the timeless values of the profession.

So, I have a challenge for you: Be that Super AI CPA. Dive deep into AI, try new things, and never forget the ethical foundations of your profession.

And hey, if you end up creating that billion-dollar AI accounting tool, remember your old professor who pointed you down this path. A small finder's fee or donation to Lehigh University would be much appreciated! (wink/wink)

In all seriousness, the future of AI in accounting is incredibly exciting, but it's also full of challenges. By sticking to the principles we've talked about – setting clear ethical guidelines, putting up smart guardrails, and always focusing on trust and verification – we can make AI a powerful force for good in accounting and in society at large.

Advice from CPA Jeffrey:

"I just want to emphasize one last point about the ethics of AI. We're going to be facing some serious temptations in the years to come. Just because AI makes something possible doesn't mean it's the right thing to do.

For instance, let's say you're reviewing a representation letter from a company's board of directors. AI might give you the capability to do a deep background check on every board member – their drinking habits, gambling history, you name it. But is that really necessary or ethical? Where do we draw the line?

It's going to be a slippery slope. As human beings, we've got to hold the line and remember our ethical obligations. AI is an amazing tool, but like any powerful technology, it can be a double-edged sword. We've got to stay vigilant and always put our professional integrity first."

13

Congratulations on Understanding AI and Becoming a Super AI CPA

CONGRATULATIONS! You've just finished a whirlwind tour of artificial intelligence that puts you miles ahead of most professionals out there – even some of the tech whizzes. But more importantly, you've gained a unique perspective on AI that's incredibly valuable in today's fast-changing world.

You're not just accountants anymore – you're Super AI CPAs. But what does that really mean?

The Super AI CPA: A New Kind of Professional

Here's a rundown of the superpowers you've picked up from this book:

1. Deep understanding of AI – not just how to use it, but how it works

2. Ability to look at AI systems with a critical eye and spot their strengths and weaknesses

3. Strong ethical grounding to guide responsible AI development and use

4. Interdisciplinary thinking – connecting ideas from different fields

5. Creative problem-solving skills to imagine new AI applications in accounting

6. Commitment to continuous learning as AI keeps changing

7. Ethical advocacy for responsible AI use and development of ethical frameworks

8. Trust and verification expertise applied to AI systems

What sets you apart now isn't just knowledge of the latest AI tools – though that's certainly part of it – it's that you can see AI through a different lens. And that lens mixes tech know-how with the wisdom you've earned as accountants.

13 | CONGRATULATIONS ON BECOMING A SUPER AI CPA

You have now gained an understanding of AI that goes beyond those courses that just teach you which buttons to push on the latest AI software. Let's recap what you've learned, because it's impressive:

AI is More Than Just a Smart Computer Program

First off, you now understand that AI isn't just a fancy calculator. It's a deep learning machine that's trying to replicate the most complicated thing we know – the human mind. That's a pretty big goal!

You've seen how AI can crunch numbers faster than any human and spot patterns in huge amounts of data. But you also know its weak spots. Those include how AI can say things that sound right but are totally wrong or make decisions based on biased data. You know that AI, as impressive as it is, still can't match the deep understanding and emotional smarts that humans have.

The Building Blocks of AI

You understand that at the heart of many of today's most impressive AI tools are large language models and generative AI. These are systems trained on tons of data that can write human-like text, analyze complex documents, and even generate creative content.

You know AI's strengths (processing information at superhuman speeds) and its weaknesses ("hallucinations" and biased outputs). More importantly, you understand that these big language models aren't the final word on AI. They are just the latest step in a long journey of trying to create machine intelligence. Who knows what the next big breakthrough will be?

Thinking Deep About Intelligence

Remember when we talked about memory, rational thinking, learning, consciousness, and even the concept of wisdom? You understand that AI is an attempt to mimic human intelligence. And because you've really thought about what intelligence and consciousness are, you have insights that many tech experts lack. You now have a way of thinking about intelligence that goes beyond IQ scores or being good at chess.

You know that real intelligence isn't just about processing power or analyzing data. It's also about creativity, emotional understanding, and wisdom. This helps you see where AI excels and where it falls short. You know that while AI can beat humans at specific, well-defined tasks, it still has trouble with the kind of general intelligence that lets a human handle the complexities of the real world.

The Historical Context

You've gained an appreciation for the long arc of AI development, from the early rule-based systems to today's deep learning models. You understand that AI didn't just appear out of nowhere in some Silicon Valley lab, but is the result of decades of work by people in many different fields.

13 | CONGRATULATIONS ON BECOMING A SUPER AI CPA

You know that many of the ideas behind today's AI breakthroughs have been around for decades, and that progress often comes in fits and starts. This historical perspective helps you tell the difference between real breakthroughs and marketing hype.

It's Not Just About Tech Anymore

One of the most exciting things you've learned is that the future of AI doesn't belong solely to the computer scientists and software engineers. As AI gets smarter and starts to affect more areas of life, we need voices from a wide range of fields to guide its development. Remember when we talked about moving from the era of enlightenment to the era of entanglement? You're now working in the era of entanglement.

You can have meaningful conversations with AI developers about the technical aspects of their work. You can chat with philosophers about the nature of intelligence and consciousness. And you can advise business leaders on how AI might impact their strategies.

CPAs Have a Big Role to Play in AI

One of the most important things you've learned is that CPAs have a unique and vital role to play in developing AI. Why? Because of two magic words we've hammered home throughout this book: trust and verification.

CPAs ensure the accuracy and integrity of financial information. You're the guardians of trust in the business world. In a time when AI is making more and more important decisions, we need professionals who can audit these systems, validate their outputs, and ensure they're operating ethically and accurately.

You've learned how to talk with tech professionals without fear or intimidation. You know enough about the fundamental concepts to ask tough questions and challenge assumptions. When someone tries to dazzle you with technical jargon, you can cut through the noise and focus on what really matters: Can we trust this AI system? Is it accurate? Does it line up with human values?

An Ethical Framework

We've spent a lot of time talking about ethics, and for good reason. As AI gets more powerful, the ethical stakes get higher. You understand that powerful technology needs equally strong ethical guardrails.

This ethical grounding is what separates a true Super AI CPA from someone who just knows how to use AI tools. You're not just asking "Can we do this with AI?" but "Should we do this with AI?"

As Super AI CPAs, you're in a unique position to help shape AI ethics at all levels: individual, group, and societywide. Your personal integrity, combined with the ethical standards of the accounting profession, will help guide the development of AI in finance and beyond. And as respected professionals, you have a voice in shaping the rules and laws that will govern how AI is used.

Real-World Applications

We've looked at how AI is reshaping the accounting profession and the business world. You've seen examples of how AI can automate routine tasks, enhance fraud detection, improve risk assessment, and find deeper insights in financial data.

But more importantly, you've learned to think creatively about new ways to use AI. You're not just using AI tools, you could be the one to come up with the next big AI breakthrough in accounting.

The Importance of Human Judgment

One of the key lessons we've hammered home is that AI is a tool, not a replacement for human judgment. You understand that while AI can process huge amounts of data and spot patterns humans might miss, it still needs human oversight and interpretation.

Remember when we talked about the Twinkie company trying to sell cupcakes as part of a diabetes diet? That's the kind of nonsense you're now equipped to spot when it comes to AI. You understand that AI isn't just a neutral number-crunching tool – it's the product of the data it learns from, the goals it's given, and the culture it's created in.

This is especially important in accounting, where decisions can have big financial and legal consequences. You know that you can't just blindly trust an AI's output. You need to use your professional skepticism, double-check results, and use your human understanding of context and nuance.

The Journey Continues

So, what does all this mean? It means that you're now ready to be leaders in the AI revolution. You have the knowledge to separate AI fact from fiction, the skills to use AI tools effectively, and the ethical grounding to ensure AI is developed and used responsibly.

Now that you've almost finished this book, please don't think your AI education is complete. Because it's not! If there's one thing you should have picked up by now, it's that the field of AI is evolving fast. What's cutting-edge today might be obsolete tomorrow.

The good news? You now have the foundation to understand new developments as they emerge, to think critically about their potential, and to guide how they're used in ethical and productive ways.

In our next chapter, we'll talk about how you can keep up with the constant changes in artificial intelligence. Because remember, in the world of AI, the learning never stops. And for Super AI CPAs like you, that's not a bug. It's a feature.

Section 3

14

What's Next to Stay a Super AI CPA

DON'T GET TOO COMFORTABLE in that freshly eared Super AI CPA cape just yet! You've got the basics down, you understand the potential, and you're ready to start flexing those Super AI CPA muscles. But in the world of AI, if you're not moving forward, you're falling behind. In this chapter, we're going to talk about staying ahead of the AI curve and keeping yourself at the cutting edge of this technology.

First things first: you signed up for a lifelong learning adventure. As we've discussed, the AI you're using right now is probably the worst one you'll ever use – it's only going to get better and smarter from here on out. If you want to stay on top of your game, you've got to keep learning, keep adapting, and keep pushing yourself.

So, how do you keep up? We've got a three-part game plan for you: continuous learning, looking for future changes, and experimentation.

The Importance of Continuous Learning

Just like you keep up with changes in tax law or accounting standards, you've got to stay on top of what's happening in AI.

Reading Books: The Classic Approach

Don't underestimate the power of good old-fashioned books for deep dives that you can't get from a quick Google search or a YouTube video.

Don't just go for the "how-to" books. Look for ones that talk about what AI means for society, where it might be heading, and all the questions it brings up.

If there's one book that I'd recommend right now, it's Ethan Mollick's *Co-Intelligence: Living and Working with AI*. It's an easy read and it will get you excited about AI. It covers many of the principles we've talked about throughout this book, in a simple and relatable way. Whether you're new to AI or looking to learn more, this book is a great choice. But this recommendation will probably change quickly.

Take Some Classes

I'm not just saying this because I teach them – though my courses are pretty good! Classes are great because they give you a clear path to follow and often give you hands-on experience with the latest AI tools.

Look for online courses, webinars, and workshops that dive into specific ways to use AI. Universities, professional organizations, and even tech companies are constantly offering new learning opportunities. In your continuing education area, our regular 3-6-month updates on Artificial Intelligence for CPAs are meant to keep you up to date and are worth a try.

And don't just stick to business classes – branch out! Try a data science course, or one on the philosophy of AI. Remember, the more you know about different AI fields, the more creative you can be with AI in your work.

Keeping Up with the Pulse of AI Through Blogs and Newsletters

Blogs and newsletters are perfect for keeping up with what's happening day-to-day in AI. They're where you'll hear about the latest breakthroughs, the emerging trends, and the hot debates everyone's talking about.

Here are three go-to bloggers that I think every aspiring Super AI CPA should follow:

1. Gary Marcus: This guy is like the grumpy old man of AI (in the best possible way). He's skeptical, he's critical, and he's not afraid to point out the emperor's (lack of)

new clothes. Marcus is great at pointing out limitations or where AI might go wrong. For instance, he's been vocal about the problems of bias in AI, the limitations of deep learning, and the potential impact of widespread AI adoption. Reading his blog is like getting a reality check – it'll keep you from getting too carried away with the AI hype.

2. Andrew Ng: On the flip side, we've got Andrew Ng. This guy is an eternal optimist when it comes to AI. He believes in AI's potential to transform various industries. Reading Ng's blog is like getting a glimpse into a sci-fi future where AI solves all our problems. Following him will keep you excited about the potential of AI and open your eyes to opportunities you might not have thought of. Plus, he's great at explaining complicated AI concepts in simple terms.

3. Ethan Mollick: He is your go-to guy for practical, real-world examples of how AI is being used right now. What sets him apart is his emphasis on experimentation. He doesn't just talk about AI he rolls up his sleeves and tries things out. His blog is full of real-world examples you can actually use, often with step-by-step guides.

The key here is balance. Read the skeptics and the optimists. Look at the big ideas and the practical, everyday uses. Keep an open mind, but don't believe everything you read.

Look Ahead: What's Coming Next?

As a Super AI CPA, you need to be thinking about what's next. So, let's talk about the future. One thing I'm pretty sure about: the current darlings of the AI world, generative language models, aren't going to be the be-all and end-all. They're impressive, but they've got some serious limitations, especially when it comes to mimicking emotions and understanding context.

I've got a hunch that we're going to see new foundations of AI in the coming years. We don't know what's coming, but we know it's coming fast.

Your job is to keep an eye out for these new ideas. Follow what's happening at universities and AI labs. Pay attention to startups working on wild new AI ideas. The next big thing in AI might be cooking up in somebody's garage right now!

Experiment, Experiment, Experiment!

Reading about AI is great, but to really get it, you need to play with it. I'm talking about good old-fashioned experimentation.

A big mistake I see people make is getting stuck in a rut with AI. They find one way to use it that works, and they just keep doing that over and over. That's a surefire way to get left behind.

Instead, make it a habit to try out new AI tools and techniques regularly. You've figured out how to use AI to make audits easier? Great! But don't stop there. How could you use it for financial forecasting? For risk assessment? For client communication?

Not every experiment will be a success, and that's okay! In fact, the things that don't work often teach us the most. If an AI tool doesn't do what you expect, dig into why. Was it a limitation of the technology? Or did you use it in the wrong way? The more you learn from these hiccups, the better you will get at using AI.

The point is to stay curious and keep pushing the limits. Try new tools, test different prompts, explore various AI approaches. The more you experiment, the better you'll understand the capabilities and limitations of these systems.

The Human Touch in a World of Algorithms

As you dive deeper into the world of AI, don't lose sight of your humanity. Treat artificial intelligence like it's human. But, as we discussed in chapter 4, always remember that you're the real human in the room.

When you're interacting with AI tools, treat them like a very smart, but sometimes confused, colleague. Question it. Challenge it.

AI is a tool to help you make decisions, not to make them for you. Your judgment, your ethics, your understanding of the big picture – these human powers are more important than ever in the age of AI.

It's not just about avoiding mistakes. It's about using the best of both worlds – human and artificial intelligence. AI can crunch huge amounts of data and spot patterns faster than any human. But you, with all your experience and sharp professional judgment, can add context, nuance, and ethical thinking that AI just can't match.

In other words, don't try to compete with AI – team up with it. Use it to make your own abilities even stronger, not to replace them. That's the true superpower of a Super AI CPA.

Supercharge with Collaboration

One of the best ways to keep up with AI is to talk to other people about it. Share your experiences, your successes, and yes, even your failures. Have you discovered a cool new way to use AI in your work? Don't keep it to yourself. Share it with your colleagues. Better yet, teach them how to do it themselves.

And it goes both ways. Listen to what others are doing. Ask your colleagues how they're using AI. What new tools have they tried? What problems have they run into? What surprised them?

Don't just stick to the accounting world either. Chat with data scientists, software engineers, ethicists – anyone working with AI. Remember, some of the best new ideas come from mixing ideas from different fields.

A Never-Ending Adventure

Staying on top of AI developments might sound like a lot of work. Things are changing so fast, and there's always something new to learn. But this is also an incredibly exciting time to be a CPA.

AI can free you from boring, repetitive tasks, letting you focus on higher-level strategic work. It can help find insights you'd never spot on your own. It can make you faster, more accurate, and more valuable to your clients than ever before.

But to make the most of it, you need to think a little differently. You need to commit to keep learning, be willing to try new things, and to be okay with sometimes failing. You need to be open to new ideas while sticking to the ethical principles that have always guided your profession.

You've taken the first step by becoming a Super AI CPA. Now it's up to you to maintain your superpower. Keep learning. Keep experimenting. Stay curious. And above all, never forget that it's your humanity that makes you irreplaceable.

15

Final Thoughts

WHEN I FIRST STARTED TEACHING about artificial intelligence, I never thought CPAs would be such big players in its development. But the more I've explored AI's strengths and weaknesses, the clearer it has become that you are exactly what the AI world needs.

Trust and Verification: The CPA's Superpower

How many times have you heard me say "trust and verification" in this book? I bet you've lost count! But there's a good reason I keep hammering this point. These two concepts make people feel confident about what CPAs do in business. And that's exactly what's needed to help everyone feel comfortable about AI in business and everyday life.

As AI becomes less about computer science and coding, and more about working with humans and helping them do their jobs better, we need people who can make sure that AI is trustworthy and ethical. We need a group that really understands how businesses and people work, not just how computers work. Sound familiar? That's you, my Super AI CPAs!

Bringing Humanity to AI

For too long, we've been missing that trustworthy voice in technology. We don't need more programmers. What we need are people who can look at AI with fresh eyes, who can ask the right questions, and who can make sure AI is doing what it is supposed to do.

That's where you come in. You're already experts at digging into complicated systems, spotting inconsistencies, and making sure everything adds up. You know how to balance innovation with responsibility. You understand the importance of ethics in business. These skills are going to be incredibly valuable as AI becomes a bigger part of our world.

15 | FINAL THOUGHTS

I see CPAs getting deeply involved with AI at every level. It starts by understanding AI from an unbiased perspective – not just the hype, not just the tech talk, but the real deal. That's what this book has been all about.

Now, you need to stay on top of new developments in AI. It's moving fast, but I know you're up for the challenge. Most importantly, you need to jump into the big discussions about AI. Where should it be used? How do we keep it ethical? What are the risks and opportunities? Your voice needs to be heard in these conversations.

A Bright Future for AI-Empowered CPAs

Close your eyes and imagine the future with me. Picture senators calling you up to get your take on AI regulations. Imagine CEOs seeking your advice on how to use AI in their companies ethically and effectively. Maybe even presidents asking what you think about national AI strategies. Sounds far-fetched? I don't think so. In fact, I believe it's right around the corner. People won't just want your take on financial matters, they'll want to know what you think AI means for business and society.

Why? Because you've got the perfect mix of skills. You understand business inside and out. You know how to verify information and build trust. And you've got a strong ethical code that guides everything you do.

As AI becomes a bigger part of business and everyday life, we need that level of trust and accountability. We need professionals who can look under the hood of AI systems, make sure they're doing what they're supposed to, and raise the alarm if something's not right. People who can make sure AI is not just clever, but trustworthy.

Don't wait for others to define AI's future – help steer it in a direction that aligns with the values of your profession. You have the power to ensure that as AI gets smarter, it will also get wiser and more ethical. That's no small task, but I know you're up for the challenge.

I firmly believe that as more CPAs evolve into Super AI CPAs, some of you will become superstars. Not only will you reap significant financial rewards, but you will also have the satisfaction of knowing you have contributed to changing the world for the better through the responsible use of AI.

The Super AI CPA

Becoming a Super AI CPA isn't just about learning to use new AI tools. It's about reimagining the entire role of CPAs in a world shaped by AI. It means stepping into new areas and sometimes pushing yourself out of your comfort zone.

You'll be the bridge between the technical world of AI and the practical, human world of business. You will help develop frameworks for auditing AI systems, create standards for AI transparency and accountability, and ensure that AI enhances human capabilities without compromising our values.

This isn't just good for the accounting profession – it's needed for society as a whole. With your expertise, you can help ensure that AI develops in ways that benefit everyone, not just a select few. You can help craft policies that promote

15 | FINAL THOUGHTS

innovation while protecting against misuse. You can be the voice of reason and ethics in a field that's moving lightning fast.

As we look to the future, I'm incredibly excited about the role CPAs will play in the AI revolution. AI isn't going to replace you. It's going to supercharge what you do. It will handle the routine tasks, crunch the numbers, spot the patterns. But it's you, with your judgment, ethics, and human insight, who will make sense of it all and guide the big decisions.

The Adventure Continues!

So, what's next? Well, that's up to you. The future of AI is not set in stone. It will be shaped by the choices we make and what we decide is important. As CPAs, you have an amazing opportunity – and I would argue, a responsibility – to ensure that AI develops in ways that benefit humanity and sticks to high ethical standards.

Before we say goodbye, I want to extend a personal invitation. This book might be ending, but our journey together in the world of AI is just beginning. I'd love to hear about your experiences as you explore the exciting world of AI. You can reach me at craig.gordon.ai@gmail.com.

Remember, stay curious! Keep asking questions, keep pushing boundaries, and keep imagining what's possible. The world of AI is full of incredible possibilities, and it needs your expertise now more than ever. The future isn't something that just happens to us – it's something we create together. And with your expertise, integrity, and vision, I know that the future of AI is in good hands.

Thank you for joining me on this journey. Now go out there and show the world what a Super AI CPA can do!

Acknowledgments

There is a common refrain that says, "it takes a village to raise a child." Well, I would like to add to this refrain by stating, "It took me a village to write this book." There's no way this book would have been written without the help of so many.

First, Irene Neumansky. What can I say Irene except no way this book gets done without you. Almost 30 years together in various ways, but it has always been true that if it needs getting done, Irene can do it! Thanks for all the work with chatbots, illustrations and editing. Sometimes I thought you should be the author, not me.

Next, Jeffrey Yudkoff, who has always been my co-conspirator in new ventures and crazy ideas. Thankfully, the crazy ideas and ventures that failed never stopped us from coming up with more crazy ideas that we could try. The possibly that we could succeed again was always the goal. We've had a couple of successes, and I hope this is one more. Thanks for the crazy idea of teaching Artificial Intelligence to CPA's.

Jay Schimmel is our third partner in this crazy idea. He's one of those wonderful friends who never stops grinding. As Jay taught me, in business and personal journeys, make sure you know who you want in the foxhole with you when trouble happens. I will always look for the foxhole that you are in.

Sharen Kindel, my copy and fact check editor. Believe it or not, her late husband was a co-editor of the first book that I did in

2001. When he passed away, I thought I would never find someone as good as him to work with again. Sharen, I was wrong. My apologies. Great job.

The following people fall under the Lehigh "mafia" connection. First, Jack Lule, who pushed me to teach Artificial Intelligence to non-tech Lehigh journalism students back in 2017, It's hard to believe today, but the academic journalism community didn't embrace AI until it was presented in working sessions at the World Journalism Education Conference (WJEC) in Paris in 2019. Due to your thinking Jack, Lehigh was one of the first colleges to realize that AI needs to be taught outside of the computer science department. How lucky was I that you were there.

Ariana Dimitrakis. When I asked Jack for a graduating student who could help in my ventures, I think he blurted out your name before my sentence was even finished. And boy was he right. You kept everything we did for this book at an excellent level.

Bill Gaudelli. I first met Bill when we were working with students attending Lehigh's Start-up Academy summer program based in San Francisco. We taught them the value of being at the cutting edge of the tech approach to journalism. That's when I met this ex-Columbia University education department head who really wanted to innovate and change the world with Lehigh, his new university, at the forefront. Thanks for all your support at Lehigh. I can't wait to see what you have up your sleeve next.

ACKNOWLEDGMENTS

Finally Kelly Stazi, Brain Creech, Matt Veto, Kathy Throne and Jeremey Littau to name a few Lehigh people who allowed me to guest lecture and get things done when I needed help. You folks make Lehigh great.

A few more from the village and then I have to stop and apologize if I missed anybody. David Franklin, one of the best researchers I have ever worked with, and CJ the DJ Skender, a classmate of mine at Lehigh who went on to become a legend teaching accounting at UNC and Duke. Joel Podolny, former dean of the Yale School of Management, founding Dean of Apple University and now trying to change the education world for the better with his new firm Honor Education. Thank you. I am here to help you all, in any way possible.

And then the folks on the sidelines that probably don't even know that they helped. Jennifer Joss, Julianne Soteriou, Richie Gordon, Karen Amestoy, Erica Franklin, Dallas Basha, Aidan Lewis, Diane Franklin, Geoff Gordon and my two doggie kids Tessie and Keiko. All of you in some way asked the right questions, just listened or let me escape the doldrum of writing without quitting many times. Thank you, woof woof!

My wish for this book? That thousands of CPA's start to understand how AI can help businesses without compromising ethical principles and lead us to better businesses for all.

Thank you very much. My very best,
Craig Gordon
October 2024

Notes

Illustrations were generated using Adobe FireFly and Midjourney

Ask the AI sections were generated using ChatGPT

Preface |
The Urgent Call for CPAs in the Age of AI

1. As Stanford professor James Landay puts it, "If a system makes a mistake…" https://hai.stanford.edu/news/davos-2024-six-takeaways-ai-conversation-wef

2. As Jensen Huang, the visionary CEO of NVIDIA, recently observed, "Deep learning is a method…" https://www.newyorker.com/magazine/2023/12/04/how-jensen-huangs-nvidia-is-powering-the-ai-revolution

3   IBM's global managing partner for generative AI, Matthew Candy, told Fortune that AI would make it much easier for people without technical skills to build products. "The speed at which people will be able to come up with an idea, to test the idea, to make something, it's going to be so accelerated."
    https://fortune.com/europe/2023/12/30/want-a-tech-job-in-2024-make-your-new-years-resolution-to-master-liberal-arts-and-language-ibms-ai-chief-says/

4   Enrollment in accounting programs has been plummeting...The CPA Journal, December 2023. Statistics indicate declining enrollment in accounting degree programs nationally, while business school degree enrollments and degree conferrals are growing. This declining trend is particularly worrisome because accounting degree enrollments and degree conferrals have dropped substantially, exceeding the overall drop in higher education enrollment.
    https://www.cpajournal.com/2023/12/29/accounting-education-disrupted/

5   Making accounting sexy again: The profession needs a makeover to attract newcomers. (2024, Mar 27). *The Economist.*
    https://www.economist.com/business/2024/03/27/making-accounting-sexy-again

6   Chart of "Americans' Ratings of Honesty and Ethics of Professions" Please tell me how you would rate the honesty and ethical standards of people in these different fields --

NOTES

very high, high, average, low or very low?
https://news.gallup.com/poll/467804/nurses-retain-top-ethics-rating-below-2020-high.aspx

Chapter 1 | Who We Are

[1] The algorithms that can spot cancer better than doctors. National Cancer Institute (NCI)-supported research has shown that AI imaging algorithms not only improve breast cancer detection on mammography but can also help predict long-term risk of invasive breast cancers.
https://pubmed.ncbi.nlm.nih.gov/37104728/
NCI scientists are using AI to improve cervical and prostate cancer screening.
https://www.cancer.gov/research/infrastructure/artificial-intelligence

Chapter 2 | How We Got to Teaching CPAs About AI

[1] *The Fourth Paradigm: Data-Intensive Scientific Discovery.* Microsoft Research, October 2009. Jerome P. Horwitz, a medical researcher at the Karmanos Cancer Institute in Detroit, MI synthesized azidothymidine (AZT) in 1964 as a potential cancer treatment. AZT was the first drug approved by the FDA to treat HIV/AIDS in 1987.

[2] Geoffrey Hinton, a British computer scientist, has been called "the Godfather of AI." His controversial ideas helped make advanced artificial intelligence possible.

3   Tegmark, Max. *Life 3.0: Being Human in the Age of Artificial Intelligence*. Alfred A. Knopf, 2017.

4   William Gibson quote, "The future is already here – it's just not very evenly distributed." https://quoteinvestigator.com/2012/01/24/future-has-arrived/

Chapter 3 |
Why You Should Become a Super AI CPA

1   Mollick, Ethan. *Co-Intelligence: Living and Working with AI.* Portfolio/Penguin, Random House LLC, 2024

2   Adams, Douglas. *The Hitchhiker's Guide to the Galaxy.* Arthur Barker Ltd. London, 1979. *The Hitchhiker's Guide to the Galaxy* aired for the first time as a BBC radio comedy on March 8, 1978. It has since become an international multimedia phenomenon; the six novels are widely distributed, having been translated into more than 30 languages.

3   May 2024 – Microsoft and LinkedIn, 2024 Work Trend Index on the state of AI at work. The Index shows that AI usage has nearly doubled in the past six months, reaching 75% of knowledge workers. https://news.microsoft.com/2024/05/08/microsoft-and-linkedin-release-the-2024-work-trend-index-on-the-state-of-ai-at-work/

NOTES

Chapter 4 | Why Understanding the Fundamentals of AI is Necessary

1. Tegmark, Max, *Life 3.0: Being Human in the Age of Artificial Intelligence*. Knopf, 2017

Chapter 5 | The 7 Rules for Understanding AI and Becoming a Super AI CPA!

2. Mollick, Ethan. Pages 47-62

1. Mark Twain: "history doesn't repeat itself, but it often rhymes." https://hotwhitesnow.wordpress.com/2024/04/18/history-doesnt-repeat-itself-but-it-often-rhymes/

2. Ray Kurzweil, https://www.cmple.com/learn/ray-kurzweils-most-notable-predictions-hits-and-misses

3. PICPA code of ethics https://www.picpa.org/advocacy-pipeline/professional-technical-standards/professional-ethics

Chapter 6 | Rule 1: Why CPAs Need to Understand AI

1. Twinkies® https://en.wikipedia.org/wiki/Twinkie

2. "Thanks to AI, you don't need a computer science degree to get a job at IBM anymore." https://fortune.com/europe/2023/12/30/want-a-tech-job-in-2024-make-your-new-years-resolution-to-master-liberal-arts-and-language-ibms-ai-chief-says/

Chapter 7 | Rule 2: To Understand AI, You Must Understand the Definition of Intelligence

1. Tegmark, Max
   https://www.dynatrace.com/news/blog/max-tegmark-on-artificial-intelligence

2. Socrates
   https://www.goodreads.com/author/quotes/275648.Socrates

3. Hawking, Stephen
   https://www.washingtonpost.com/news/answer-sheet/wp/2018/03/29/stephen-hawking-famously-said-intelligence-is-the-ability-to-adapt-to-change-but-did-he-really-say-it/

4. Angelou, Maya
   https://www.brainyquote.com/quotes/maya_angelou_578823

5. Einstein, Albert
   https://www.cftc.gov/PressRoom/SpeechesTestimony/opaomalia-16

6. vos Savant, Marilyn
   https://libquotes.com/marilyn-vos-savant/quote/lbs2g9p

7. How Plants Communicate
   https://www.washingtonpost.com/climate-environment/2023/10/21/plants-talk-warning-

danger/#https://www.science.org/doi/10.1126/science.aat7744

Chapter 8 | Rule 3: Today's Reality Defines Current Intelligence and History Defines Current Reality

1. Alan Turing:
   https://www.britannica.com/science/history-of-artificial-intelligence

2. Grace Hopper:
   https://president.yale.edu/biography-grace-murray-hopper

3. Claude Shannon:
   https://en.wikipedia.org/wiki/A_Mathematical_Theory_of_Communication
   https://www.quantamagazine.org/how-claude-shannons-information-theory-invented-the-future-20201222/

4. The Dartmouth Conference:
   https://home.dartmouth.edu/about/artificial-intelligence-ai-coined-dartmouth

5. ImageNet: https://www.image-net.org/about.php

6. Moore's Law:
   https://www.investopedia.com/terms/m/mooreslaw.asp

7. AlphaFold: https://alphafold.ebi.ac.uk/

8. Casey Handmer, green energy
   https://caseyhandmer.wordpress.com/2024/05/22/the-

solar-industrial-revolution-is-the-biggest-investment-opportunity-in-history/

9   Kuhn, Thomas. *The Structure of Scientific Revolutions*. The University of Chicago Press, 1962. Unprecedented connectivity between datasets has the potential to answer many scientific questions simply by connecting the dots.

10 Li, Fei-Fei. *The Worlds I See*. Flatiron Books, 2023

Chapter 9 | Rule 4: Before Using AI Tools, CPAs Must Understand their Strengths and Weaknesses

1   EY's Document Intelligence platform: https://www.ey.com/en_us/services/ai

2   Einstein: "If I had an hour to solve a problem…" https://quoteinvestigator.com/2014/05/22/solve/#google_vignette

3   Claude's Constitutional AI: https://www.anthropic.com/news/claudes-constitution

4   Cambridge Analytica Scandal: https://www.nytimes.com/2018/04/04/us/politics/cambridge-analytica-scandal-fallout.html

Chapter 11 | Rule 6: The Quest for AI Consciousness

1   Gelernter, David. *The Tides of Mind: Uncovering the Spectrum of Consciousness*. Liveright Publishing Corporation, 2016.

NOTES

2 The Turing Test: https://en.wikipedia.org/wiki/Turing_test

3 Tests for AI consciousness: https://www.science.org/content/article/if-ai-becomes-conscious-how-will-we-know

4 Fermi's Paradox: https://pages.uoregon.edu/jschombe/cosmo/lectures/lec28.html

5 Great Filter theory: https://www.astronomy.com/science/the-great-filter-a-possible-solution-to-the-fermi-paradox/

6 Bayes' theorem: https://www.geeksforgeeks.org/bayes-theorem/

Chapter 14 | What's Next to Stay a Super AI CPA

Books

Hey, Tony, et al. *The Fourth Paradigm: Data-Intensive Scientific Discovery*. Microsoft Research, 2009.

Gelernter, David. *The Tides of Mind: Uncovering the Spectrum of Consciousness*. Liveright Publishing Corporation, 2016.

Kuhn, Thomas S. *The Structure of Scientific Revolutions*. University of Chicago Press, 1962.

Li, Fei-Fei. *The Worlds I See*. Flatiron Books, 2023

Mollick, Ethan. *Co-Intelligence: Living and Working with AI*. Portfolio, 2024

Tegmark, Max. *Life 3.0: Being Human in the Age of Artificial Intelligence*. Alfred A. Knopf, 2017.

Blogs

Andrew Ng: The Batch. https://www.deeplearning.ai/the-batch/

Ethan Mollick: One Useful Thing. https://www.oneusefulthing.org/

Gary Marcus: Gary Marcus's Blog. https://garymarcus.substack.com/

Made in the USA
Columbia, SC
16 October 2024